Against Capitalist Education

Education

What is education for?

Against Capitalist Education

What is education for?

Nadim Bakhshov

Winchester, UK
Washington, USA

First published by Zero Books, 2015
Zero Books is an imprint of John Hunt Publishing Ltd., Laurel House, Station Approach,
Alresford, Hants, SO24 9JH, UK
office1@jhpbooks.net
www.johnhuntpublishing.com
www.zero-books.net

For distributor details and how to order please visit the 'Ordering' section on our website.

ISBN: 978 1 78535 057 3
Library of Congress Control Number: 2015934351

A CIP catalogue record for this book is available from the British Library.

Design: Lee Nash

Printed and bound by CPI Group (UK) Ltd, Croydon, CR0 4YY, UK

We operate a distinctive and ethical publishing philosophy in all
areas of our business, from our global network of authors to
production and worldwide distribution.

CAST

John Thoreau
George R Wells
*The conversation took place at the Borges Library, Athenaeum House,
London, Summer 2014.*

To my wife Lara and my daughters, Maya and Sofia

Preface

About 5 years ago, I read Mark Fisher's 'Capitalist Realism'. For me there was a profound question and an enormous challenge at the heart of this book: how do we create alternatives?

The book you hold is a step in thinking a response.

In the last four years I began to look for a model to present this response. I looked at the writing styles of Descartes' 'Discourses', Plato's middle dialogues, Montaigne's essays, 'pataphysics, Queneau's 'Exercises', Perec's experiments, the OULIPO, Diderot's 'Jacques', Spinoza's 'Ethics', Borges' fictions and Dante's 'Commedia'. It was out of years of experiments that I found that Montaigne's writing, as a site of effort, of trying things out, struck a chord with me. But instead of the essay form, could I use a conversational, dramatic form, a form I had developed through my own studies over a thirty year period?

Given the importance of conversation in all of our lives, the art of writing a conversation would seem natural and unproblematic. The truth is there is a real craft here. Literal transcription does not make for a pleasant reading experience. The conversation you are about to read is meant to live in your imagination and has been carefully crafted to this end.

To have a genuine revolution in this internet-saturated age, with capitalism colonising every corner of the mind and body, including the depths of the unconscious, we begin with imagination and conversation and lots of wild leaps into impossible realms. We bypass prejudices, mix ideas that don't normally go together, we start in one place then turn and head off in completely unexpected directions. We find new starting points that many very rarely think of. We abandon assumptions when we can, adopt others. We crisscross paths from all the wrong directions to discover what we might have missed.

So, let us join a small group and listen to two friends talking and discussing how to find a path out of capitalism. Listen as they circle around topics, jump from one area to another, come back later on, sometimes never return, suddenly interrupt each other, all the time trying to see something that might stir our thought and imagination, something that might trigger an image that could plant a seed of a revolution in our lives.

Nadim Bakhshov
The Lighthouse Room, 2014

Act One

Scene 1

When I came upon John Thoreau and George R Wells they were reclining on sofas in the lobby of the library with seven or so students who had already gathered around them, some I recognized from classes earlier that day, others from other universities. They were all sitting quietly, drinking, lost in thought, as if a question had been asked, or a challenge had been posed which none of them knew how to answer. I found a spare chair by the window. Through the thick frosted glass I saw people silently going about their business, the occasional black cab rushing off to its faraway destination, dodging cyclists. And just beyond the street, in the green square beyond, I found my eyes settle on the trees – oblivious to this human world, gently swaying in the autumnal winds, as if they were in a completely different time. Inside, immediately around me, the small group of students were beginning to chat, expressing some restlessness – is this going anywhere? Have we come to an end? Shouldn't we get back to halls? I manoeuvred my chair close to the edge of the cluster of sofas so I could see my friends John and George. There they were, sitting at the head of the group, lost in thought. I kept myself in the background, not wishing to be recognized nor interfere with the conversation that might unfold. John broke the silence.

John Let's just admit it's not working. Re-treading the same ground, looking for something amongst the ruins. Every time we find more withered seeds, nurture them, bring them back to life and see a possible future, it all breaks and crumbles. However hard we try to hold it, to keep it alive, we get two or three steps out and the capitalists get in our way. You have to pay for what you've found. By the time we persuade them to let us pass it's fallen apart in our hands, turned to dust. So go back, start again. Dig further down, go to the edges. You might find something no

1

one else has. You might put something new together that won't fall apart, that might make a future. But it's not working. There are so few of us left, wandering amongst the dead earth and rubble. Haven't we exhausted this place? Haven't we tried too hard to take the smallest fragment to make a whole life?

John sighed.

John Where once stood an ancient castle now lies a ruin. And they keep us here, believing there's no other way. The wild forests beyond are empty and dark, full of danger. But here? What's left? I keep on finding broken stones concealing images of the Holocaust. Fragments of an abyss, a freedom to destroy. If we leave, if we fail, then the future is destined to repeat the past – another century of wars, nuclear bombs dropped on innocent lives – another Holocaust. Can you sense it? What will it be this time? The rot in our souls? The death of our home, this planet?

At this last comment several of the students murmured their agreement.

George So, what's left?

John Abandon all those revolutionary philosophies.

George Become pragmatists? We've had a century of pragmatism. It's made us deeply subservient to orthodoxies. Nothing should challenge the system because, as the pragmatists tell us, the system works.

John Science?

George Our love for science, that child of natural philosophy, has also been perverted, corrupted. Like Faust. Sold its soul. For what? A walk-on part in a television show? Paid in blood and become a prejudice. The prejudice grown into a dogma. And now education pays to defend this dogma with a new priesthood.

John That's unfair.

George Is it? This vast labyrinthine bureaucracy grows like a sickness in us. Everyday life, when we think we worry, we fear, we hide from the minotaur. Our everyday life is neither a tragedy nor a comedy but a banal television soap, endlessly repeating the same formulas, encountering the same souls with different faces. The world is becoming more claustrophobic, more hierarchical and the layers are smothering everything. Everyone's a policeman. Everyone's policing their own behaviour. Why? There's no God to do it for us.

John Have we all become Akaky Akakievichs?

There was a pause as one of the students dropped her notes. She muttered an apology.

George Mind games at work, petty politics everywhere, detached from any real concerns. I tell you, because I know these things. It's all about perception and who you know. Instead of life we have museums of dead thought. They're springing up everywhere. A veritable festival of pointless activity. Get kitted up. We've got a dig on this week. We found a corporate sponsor. They want some archaeological research to support an investment.

George sighed, then continued.

George Out there, the planet suffocates and burns. The red weed takes root across the Earth, polluting the ocean, killing off the forests. We don't need an alien invasion. We've got capitalism. And it's in permanent crisis, co-opting or generating – not sure which – greed, fear and terror, a contagion of the spirit – flattening everything in its path. The cybernetic dream – humans as functioning economic units. Why have civilisation and education when you can have technology? Can't you feel the grip of this destructive downward movement? We want to prove we are absolutely free. So let's drag Hell up into the world. As if we're trying to prove our freedom by destroying everything that matters.

John sighed and shifted awkwardly.

John Every night my anxiety haunts my dreams, every working day of my life I sense its presence slumbering below, like some Lovecraftian monster, waiting to destroy everything I love.

George I feel the same.

John Do we need a bloody revolution?

George But under what banner?

They paused.

Scene 2

George frowned. The students began to whisper between themselves.

John I'm sick of this. All this effort wasted on critical theory. It's only part of the picture. Let's shift the axis, put some energy into telling stories. Use fiction, myths and story-telling to understand and explain the world. We've done it for centuries. Before Derrida there was Sophocles. Let's cut back critical theory. Let's read Moore's Utopia instead, chase the tail of utopian fiction through the past four hundred years. Or Gulliver's Travels? Get stuck into a satire. Better still read Balzac. I read somewhere that Marx claimed all his most important insights came from Balzac. Or Kafka and Gogol – get every school child to study the Overcoat. I know you don't think much of science fiction, but Wells, Huxley and Orwell – now there were some profound things said in their writings, writing which was also popular.

George There is, no doubt, a clear connection between fiction and the revolutionary spirit.

John But?

George But there's still a problem here. We can't change the world solely through discussions of books and films. Nor can we rely on critical theorising. With one we get caught in the subtleties of metaphor, language and imagery, with the other we get trapped in technicalities. Two different paths, each one moving away from what is needed.

John To change the world?

George Yes. To change the world. We need a path through all of this that involves fiction and critical theory but doesn't just look at the world. It generates a world. A combination of the two that –

John That what?

George That might plant the desire for a revolution in the human imagination.

Some of the students began to write. A couple got up and rushed into the library, chatting quietly and urgently to each other. We all watched them go.

The last comment hung in the air.

Scene 3

Early evening began to settle over the library. Small groups filed past, books, tablets and notepads in arms.

John Are we stuck?

George I am. Like a broken record. I keep on saying that I need to do something – I need a new path. So I'll go into the woods below the hill and find my own path. Under my arm I'll have a book. It won't be a work of academic philosophy. That won't help me where I want to go. When I'm struggling at work, some petty tyrant overseeing my work, micro-managing me, I imagine myself entering this wood, away from everyone, free, able to think. I find a clearing and open my book. And I find the writer is trying to imagine a world, a just world. It haunts him. Work ends. I go home and at the weekends I talk about films, books, critical thinkers and philosophers with friends or sometimes I sit by myself. I can't shake it off. Something in that book. It keeps on flashing through my mind. Some hint, some possibility. A revolution? But the book is odd, unusual. It is a written conversation. And in the exchange of this written conversation I find something extraordinary. A way of thinking. A way of thinking that needs the imagination. A way of thinking that simply doesn't give some worked-out plan of a just world. A way of thinking that shows itself as a shared, social activity. All in a conversation. But a written conversation? Really? Am I serious? Who writes them these days? Who writes a drama of the imagination and reason? But there's something more. What if the written conversation can open up something revolutionary...?

John Revolutionary?

Scene 4

George I have a thought. A crazy thought. I'd like to try something if you'll indulge it? Can we talk about a place, an invented place. I don't mean an alien world or a far-away utopia. What about a university? One designed on educational principles that runs counter to capitalism. One that is wired to the social, political and economic realities of our global world in a radically different way.

John An alternative university?

George How about it? We both know how discussions on the future of humanity end. In a museum of thought poring over some technical or specialised language – as if talking about change with the right words in the right order will make any difference. Or they pass the responsibility back to economics and politics. Or they give up thought. Or, for some, they abandon political change and fly off to some Californian new age guru who'll sort it all out. Round and round in circles we go, getting dizzier and dizzier, losing our balance. Every turn making promises, opening paths that are never pursued. The gap between theory and practice growing every day. We need to close this gap, find a bridge, a path between the two. Let's see if we can put flesh on alternative educational principles. See what a university might look like.

John Flesh?

George Concrete buildings, lecture rooms, seminar rooms, laboratories – yes, flesh. If we are going to imagine a university surely we're going to have to imagine the town or city it is located in? And, perhaps, the world that it exists in. But only minimally. We are not creating a whole world. We need to keep our focus narrow.

John It's quite an unusual way of conducting an argument. Build an imaginative place and university in some made-up town or city and then see how it all fits together?

George It's been attempted once before.

John Moore's Utopia?

George No. Plato's Republic.

Scene 5

A silence fell between them. One of the students to my immediate left shifted awkwardly. John glanced up at her.

John Where is this imagined university going to be?

George Here's a strange thought. Let's try and imagine it's actually out there. When we speak about it let's try and speak in the present tense. I want to make it as real as possible. Rather than get lost in the art of creating it in our conversation, even though we are creating it in our conversation. Instead let's talk as if it's out there now, in the real world.

John Well, George, that's so unusual that I think it's worth a go.

Scene 6

George So, there's a small town west of London, close to the M40 to Oxford. It's called Westhampton. If you were to draw a line straight up from Southampton you'd find it. It's less than a hundred years old. It grew out of seeking cheaper living costs for those working in the colleges of London University. There's a great train line between Westhampton and Paddington. Part of London's commuter belt. In addition to all those professors, doctors and poor research graduates it is actually populated by lots of people who service London. It's currently got a growing population of around 100,000. Okay?

John hesitated.

John You've started this crazy idea of yours, haven't you? You think we can really do this? Imagine a real alternative? Or are you going to say something even more dramatic? Are you going to say a revolutionary alternative?

George Well, that's the key question. On its own it cannot be revolutionary. But it is a start of a movement. If we imagine an education that is so radically different from what we have; if we try to visualise it out there – as if it really were there, living, breathing, trying to survive – don't you think it might lead to something?

John You're making imagination very political.

George Politics wouldn't exist without imagination.

John But if we fail?

George So what if we fail. If we don't do it because we fear failure, nothing will change. We will stay in the same state, go round the same circles, forever repeating the same mistakes and watch as our current educational systems are crushed under the force of capitalism. Is that what we want? Do we not want to try?

Do we not want a different power, a power to change, a power to transform this fragmented world into a future of peace? I for one think this is worth doing even if it is doomed from the outset. Because I want a global civilisation that brings peace to life on earth, that overcomes capitalism and re-enchants existence. Are you with me? One thing we both agree upon is the need for alternatives, not just one, but an education system that generates trillions of them – we need imagination and thought working together. We need to start this movement today.

John Then I am with you. I've got nothing better to do than give this a go.

Scene 7

George paused, looked through his notes and then continued. He seemed slightly annoyed at that last remark.

George Westhampton recently opened up its own university. Let's start by talking about its founding educational principles.

John Why start there? Why not describe the building? The physical layout? Get a feel for how it looks? Is it a campus university? Does it have its own accommodation?

George We could, but it's not the physical building that makes it radical or different.

They stopped. A group of elderly scholars walked by from reception, passing them without looking their way. John glanced up, recognised one, lifted a hand but then noticed George staring at him and withdrew. When they had passed out of view a silence fell over the group.

John I think I see your point. Out there in the so-called real world, the education system is being crushed – as you say – by the demands of capitalism and, in turn, it's crushing those who pass through it, reducing them, diminishing them. The dream of the economic functioning unit. But how do we fight it from within? It's so easy to become a career academic – learn the specialised vocabularies, accept the rules and join in. Say the right things to the right people. Get that promotion. If they question you, show them all your publications. Show them how you've contributed.

George But don't worry if you don't have any impact on real lives?

John How do you stop the system from being corrupted from within?

They paused. The student next to me began scribbling down some notes.

George We need to be honest. The wasteland is growing. There's no doubt about that. And the system is being corrupted from within. People just don't see it. We need to shine a light into the heart of things. But to do that we need a light powerful enough to show the corruption for what it is. An alternative generates a different light. That's what we need. That's the first step.

John Okay. Then continue with this crazy idea of Westhampton University.

Scene 8

George To found Westhampton University its creators went back to the root of philosophy and found a most startling thing: the beginning of the philosophical tradition started with poetry, spoken conversation and then written conversation. I'm not sure anyone would expect to find essays or academic treatises or articles. But poetry? Conversation? No one writes conversations in modern academia. They do engage with them – but the models are medieval, not classical. In the modern world of the career academic it's all articles, papers and specialised research. It has no poetry. It's more like a pale echo of modern scientific writing. And now they've turned philosophy into a private club. Only for professionals.

John Leave them to it I say.

George I don't think we should leave it to them. Our humanity is at stake here. Poetry is the closest language gets to music, and music comes from some magical place. And conversation? Spoken, it is the most natural form of human communication. The flow and exchange of thoughts, the interruptions, the disagreements, clarifications. In one form or another it's at the core of our lives. Why should we leave it to them?

John Yes, but most people think written conversations should only be found in drama – not philosophy.

George Well, Westhampton University puts it right at the centre, including the way it assesses different subjects. I know I haven't even begun talking about what courses it offers. We'll get to it. It's quite complex.

John Do teachers like working there? Has it been difficult to recruit?

George They are queuing up to work there. The thought of freedom has drawn them there. It aspires to be everything we want from our universities – places of imagination, discovery and stimulation –, where research is something new. How can I put it? A bit like Goethe's idea of science – it is generative and collaborative.

John I take it Westhampton University challenges the typical departmental structure?

George In time. Let's push on.

Scene 9

One of the librarians at the desk wandered over to the group and paused. Everyone stopped and turned to her and, as if the courage had failed her, she smiled awkwardly and returned to the desk on the other side of the marbled lobby.

George I see a withered, dying figure, haunting the ruins of a mausoleum, hiding, feeding off dead thoughts it finds amongst the broken stones. It has become a parasite. Where once there was dignity and freedom there is only a shadowy presence, not even an absence. But it is not alone. If you wait you will see it gather out of sight with others. And if you approach you can hear them whisper in obscure languages that no one can understand, inventing unintelligible gestures, cynically generating more complexity, more theoretical configurations. Amongst them I hear one with a familiar French accent, holding forth, talking slowly and with dignity but corrupted from within, slowly tearing out the heart of the tradition he belongs to. Philosophy is the hand that is erasing itself. Emptying itself of its intrinsic power. These figures gather and lure in young men and women, who come to them ever-hopeful for a just society, one free of capitalist corruption. These withered figures paralyse them with their intellects and then infect them, filling their bodies with words no one has heard before, gestures that seem revolutionary, and a burning anger that obscures the light in their minds. So I wander out into the daylight, into the citadels of imagination and fiction. I am dazzled by the bright surfaces, overwhelmed by the masses gathered to watch the spectacles generated by the writers and poets. I see a poet performing on a corner, a small crowd applauding the flow of images that pour from her page. I see a writer, sitting under camera lights, being interviewed, discussing his latest work, a crowd laughing and smiling. Everywhere people are talking, watching films, reading and absorbed in digital screens. I find the noise unbearable and turn into an alley round the back from this place. And there I find nothing. No buildings. A few workers maintaining the thin surfaces and wires everywhere, pouring electricity into our minds. The writers and poets are out there, caught in the spectacle. Like some hallucinatory buzz they cannot leave the stage, the attention, the bright colours and sounds. The plots they generate are getting more complex, the characters less so. They are addicted to the spectacle. How can we tear them away from this and tell them we need them to create different fictions?

John Is that what holds this fragmented, passive education system in place? We put the serious thinkers in a university and get them to specialise – get lost in labyrinthine and endless critical work. Then co-opt the writers, poets and dramatists to generate or write beautifully constructed award winning literature that creates shiny and glittery surfaces to hypnotise the ordinary public? Each builds a career and becomes important, while the humanity they serve begins to fade.

George But they never come together. The thinkers are lost in the dusty corridors of museums of thought. The poets are physically wired into citadels of spectacle.

John Who asks them to come together?

George paused and seemed momentarily confused.

George I do. Look, it's not that we don't have public thinkers or great writers – there are a few and I admire them enormously. But there's nothing in our ordinary education to keep them together. Schooling indoctrinates youngsters into the world without challenging it, without imagining alternatives. It is a claustrophobic, cramped place to be in, and with every new initiative getting further mired in different dead-ends. And teachers are, of course, nobodies. Their social status is lower than bankers. In the news you hear people arguing how important bankers are for our social, political and economic well-being, how banking bonuses are necessary to keep the best. But you can pay teachers a pittance and they'll be as good as anyone else – because anyone can teach. Meanwhile, in the real world, our education fails to be a civilising force.

John What do you need civilisation for if you've got technology?

Scene 10

George What I need is civilisation, a peaceful global civilisation. And to get one I need to do something strange and a bit unusual. Admittedly, it doesn't help that what Plato did was stranger still. In Book 2 of the Republic. A moment in the history of human consciousness when an educational revolution was born – and then lost and forgotten.

John What actually did he do? What was this thing that impresses you?

George sipped his water before speaking.

George Here's the scene. Socrates has been arguing with a certain Thrasymachus, a young aristocrat – extremely arrogant and unpleasant. They have been arguing about political justice, and Socrates has not been very convincing.

John I thought Socrates won everything?

George Actually he pretty much loses most of the time. Socrates tries his usual tricks but gets nowhere. His opponent is rude and sharp, and suggests Socrates is deluded – don't be ridiculous Socrates, might is right, it has always been the case and will carry on being the case. Justice belongs to the rulers, the winners. By the end of Book 1 of The Republic Socrates has failed. Plato is not ashamed to show us that his arguments have been disappointing. His friends aren't too pleased. But it doesn't end there. They ask him to defend justice in his own way – they want to give him another chance.

John What kind of chance?

George To present justice in any way he likes. Instead of analysing society or constructing abstract arguments, do something different. Now, here's a question: Did Plato make all of this up? Did he stage this moment so he could write something never written before? Did he let Socrates fail so we could move in a different direction? A direction that Plato sensed was potentially revolutionary?

John So what does he do?

George He gives up the usual argumentative stuff we're used to hearing from him, picking apart what words mean. He says: let's try to bring a city to life in the imagination, a city which embodies justice. And then let's see what that would be like. The funny thing is we can't be sure the real Socrates ever actually tried such a thing. We can't be sure that this conversation actually ever took place. It becomes a pure fiction crafted by Plato. And like all fiction, it is crafted with great poetic, dramatic and philosophical care. But why write it as a fictional conversation? A conversation which invents a just city in the imagination?

John I once tried to transcribe a conversation and realised that a verbatim copy is almost meaningless, full of half-sentences, broken lines of thought, changes of direction and endless interruption. It's not that easy to write a conversation. And most people aren't used to reading them.

George I agree. It requires a poetic sensibility to balance all the elements, to get the images right, the interaction, to feel real and to let the reader be drawn into it.

John How did he manage to juggle all those elements?

George Perhaps he was, as some say, starting from a deeper ground.

John A deeper ground?

George Yes.

Scene 11

John Did anyone continue in this strange tradition of writing philosophy in conversations?

George Not many. Aristotle, his greatest student – and another great philosopher – tried. It didn't suit him. He was more what we might call scientific, less concerned with the poetic and literary. Instead of conversations, he invented the lecture and created a style more familiar to modern academia. In fact most of the medieval period of philosophy followed Aristotle, not Plato. I suppose you might add David Hume and George Berkeley, who both wrote short conversational works. Diderot also writes in a strange hybrid form, something between ordinary prose fiction and written conversation. But these written conversations, although important, were very limited. Hume was perhaps one of the best writers amongst them, but you wonder how much effort it took to craft his fiction as opposed to work on the philosophy. Compared to essays, articles and treatises, conversations have remained fairly marginal, but for us they are there at the birth of philosophy, alongside the Pre-Socratic poet-philosophers.

John Why was Plato so different?

George He was a different type of human being, one who moved freely in the company of a Sophocles and Euripides as well as Socrates. He knew that conversation needed crafting – not dissimilar to the way a drama is written. Unlike many who have come after him, his genius, like his name, was broad. He was a mathematician and poet. It's interesting that the craft of writing conversation to explore, elucidate and develop thoughts is something many people ignore when they think of Plato. The actual conversational form is essential to the birth of philosophy. To stage a conversation, put fleshly detail on this setting – and then discuss deep and profound issues about life – that is always new. Even to us. Not only does it do something more, but at the same time it demands something more from both writers and readers of conversation and dialogue. And education doesn't encourage the writing of conversation and dialogue.

John Have we lost something?

George We constantly break up the human into a logical side and a poetic side. What we don't want are thinkers who can also use their imagination. Or imaginative people who really think. Now they would be a problem. They would see what the rest of us don't. For them, the imagination is not an escape. It's a view into the inward depth of our lives and the world – when it operates properly. Thanks largely to the entertainment industry the imagination has become dysfunctional – obsessed with shadows and echoes of reality and unable to separate its own activities from the world around it. Westhampton University is founded on the principle that both sides need to be developed in all human beings. It seeks a revolutionary change in human civilisation by putting the combined force of logic and poetry to a singular purpose. That's the education Westhampton University is offering.

Scene 12

John How did people read him? Was it just a Utopian fantasy? Did anyone actually try to build Plato's just city?

George I doubt it. Part of the reason I am still impressed with him is that I believe this written conversation is a forgotten method. We can construct revolutionary worlds through it because we're not beholden to the stylistic limits of an essay or treatise. We can explore the meaning of these revolutionary realities as freely as we need – chasing down every implication in the most natural way we find. We're not obliged to adopt a technical vocabulary that would alienate everyone except those trained in academia. Revolution and conversation belong to humanity. A trillion conversations imagining new realities and then thinking them – all going on in Westhampton University. In our internet saturated reality the spread of revolution could be viral. The networks are already in place. Ignite one of them and the idea will spread like a virus, infecting everyone.

John That goes against the grain a bit, doesn't it? Wasn't Plato a totalitarian or fascist? Why would anything he write support a revolution?

George That's a lie. It is a measure of our spiritual ruin. It helps make us all a lot less human and the systems more barbaric. A proper sense of what philosophy is, or should be, has been eroded and diminished. To accuse him of fascism or totalitarianism is to miss the point. There's something sinister and – dare I say – useful in rejecting him. At Westhampton there's a series of annual public lectures around the politics of late-capitalism. How it cleverly rejects access to the depth of the philosophical and literary tradition. These lectures present a different Plato. A man who brought the craft of written conversation into the world. A man who explored his own views through it – even though the written dialogues and conversations helped rip apart his own certainties.

John You speak as if you've been to Westhampton.

George Only in my imagination.

Scene 13

John But what is philosophy?

George Well, let's start with what it isn't. It's not pseudo-science. Nor is it parasitic on other disciplines. It is, in its heart, generative.

It creates realities. Logic and reason come into force only if imagination is there. You might disagree, but if you keep them apart you might as well program a computer to spin disks with carefully selected words to generate random combinations and call it a thinking machine. We've allowed philosophy to be ripped apart and its flesh consumed by its offspring. Science has torn reason from imagination and love, and has strapped it to experimentation and data. Art has stolen the imagination and left love to capitalism. And the fanatics are quietly corrupting religion. Westhampton University is trying to revive the corpse of philosophy, even though everywhere else it is rotting. There's real work to be done.

John Rotting?

George You can sense it. Each of us yearns for unity and meaning and justice. We want to connect to our life, to touch the wonder at its root and to live in a world that is not governed by petty tyrants, be they people or our systems. When it is not there we can sense its absence. There is a pain there. You might ask: why can't poetry restore our humanity, open up alternatives? It can, but only if it forges an intimate relationship with its poet-philosopher ancestors and joins Westhampton in creating a new type of drama: a drama of ideas, a drama where philosophy returns home.

The student next to me wrote some more notes.

John It's getting late. Shall we stop? Can I try and capture what I understand we've been talking about?

George Sure.

John All revolutions are born of a yearning that grows out of this absence. It's all about imagining worlds, societies, institutions. But not simply as escapist fiction, or entertainment – but as a way of thinking, as a form of revolutionary art. An art that can conjure up possibilities to break us out of this – how would you put it?

George This modern malaise, where mediocrity sits at the top table and leaders are tyrants who mask their limitations with airs and graces of self-importance, and quietly, without being resisted, remove the obstacles and allow capitalism in.

John Yes.

They stopped suddenly. The conversation seemed to lead to silence. George looked upset, got up and went into the library. One of the students quietly got up and put his notes down in his place. He whispered something to the girl next to him. A moment later another student got up – time for a quick break. Several students quickly disappeared. John got up and walked out of the library with a few students.

Act Two

Scene 1

I found myself in the momentary peace of my own solitude. In the silence of the library entrance, with its high ceiling and sense of history and tradition – I found myself drifting off. I was in a busy eighteenth century pub. A lonely figure, sitting and eating all by myself. The rest of the pub was buzzing around me. I looked up and a softly spoken mendicant approached, telling me I had a duty, a spiritual duty to bring something into the world to help heal it and save humanity from the abyss of self and planetary destruction.

I woke with a start.

The students had begun to return and sit back down. I turned to the window. The sun was setting on this warm autumnal evening, the streaks of orange and red were flowing up from behind the park like a gigantic planetarium show.

George returned with books under one arm. John strode back in from the outside with the same students. Someone coughed. I turned away, keeping myself hidden. Most people had returned.

John Was Plato's path really to invent a city in the imagination? To conjure up its principles, ideals and organisation through words and conversation?

George A city in the imagination. Yes. And he used his written conversations to develop a new institution. One that had never existed before.

John Are you serious? Using written conversations? What institution?

George The first university in the history of humanity – the

Academy. This is why Westhampton is returning to Plato for inspiration. Using the imagination to generate fictions which then reason and thought apply themselves to. That's a core design principle of the education at Westhampton. And, like Plato, these fictions that are constructed are not written as modern academic papers – as if everything had been worked out already and simply needed to be applied.

John And that is what inspires you?

George Yes. And the leaders of Westhampton University.

Scene 2

John I know we've mentioned this before but it keeps on nagging me. Out there, in our world, most people haven't heard of Plato, and if they have, they tend to see him as one of the first totalitarian thinkers – proto-fascist or communist – someone who we should not study anymore, who we should avoid. Some people have even linked Plato to a form of religious absolutism – one that has become closely associated with terrorism in our time.

George What you've described, these ideological distortions and lies, allow us to remain asleep. He was not a proto-fascist or communist. He wasn't simply spelling out a fixed and established set of beliefs. Through his written conversations – or dialogues as most people call them – he found ways of exploring and challenging his own ideas, that is undeniable. That was all.

John Then why do so many people believe it?

George Because it's taught that way. I don't know. Because he believed in a philosophical aristocracy. And the idea is difficult for us. But I don't have to share his belief in a philosophical aristocracy, do I? You're saying: if I'm going to read and study him I implicitly agree with him. Why should that be so? I don't share these aristocratic beliefs, but that's no reason to stop reading him. Unless you can find me someone else with his depth, imagination and writing? But we both know it. No one else writes like he does, mixes myth and logic and wild speculations and a desire for a just world in quite the same way. If we surrender him, put him back on the shelf of some dusty library in some forgotten museum of thought, we erase him. We also cancel the revolutionary kernel in his thought. And we erase a possibility of what it means to be human.

John Then what do you believe in?

George I believe in a philosophical democracy – I believe in the necessity of community and exchange. I believe democracy is unstable – and as Plato said – liable to corruption, liable to end up in an oligarchy or tyranny. To protect it we need to revive this undead corpse of philosophy and give its dignity back. We need to raise the status of teaching above that of bankers. And we need to find alternative ways of organising and thinking about education and what it's for. If we don't, well...

Scene 3

George paused, but John remained silent, lost in thought. Then quietly, as if he was testing out words, John spoke:

John How true are our modern forms of education to Plato's Academy? How do our ambitions compare to the ambition of Plato's Republic? Do we still have a fundamental philosophic core in our system? And what about Westhampton? Will it be forced to become a commercial university, charging exorbitant fees while it exhorts us to be idealistic?

George Westhampton is vulnerable. You're right. To want an alternative education system means that we have to protect and nurture it. Which means protecting it from the capitalists. Like a new species, we need to feed and take care of it, allow it time to grow and mature, to allow short-term failures not to obscure long term revolutionary ambitions. Leave it alone. Stop picking flowers before they are fully formed. Stop breaking off fruit before it has ripened. Give it time. Even if this time is for our shared imagination.

Out of the corner of my eye I noticed the street lamps, now white, almost imperceptibly switch on.

John There's a feeling that we have failed – not you and me, but all of us. For the capitalist machinery education can be nothing more than training. The profound philosophical desire for knowledge, understanding and meaning is being rewired out of the system. The technocrats who are doing this are standing as celebrities, spewing out their neoliberal ideologies masked as a genuine urge for a better education. According to them, under-standing and meaning are purely functional, overrated epiphe-nomena of evolution and brain activity. Once we're all rewired we won't feel a thing. In fact the word education might one day be erased by newspeak bureaucrats – the career academics.

George Even science loses itself in the fight for funding and status.

John What worries me is that the philosophical activity in Plato's Republic, the one we want to emulate, becomes almost impos-sible in our modern system. The belief that education, politics and the economy are the best we can hope for is driving us to surrender our humanity, our imagination and soul, and we are slowly degenerating into amorphous, distorted images of ourselves, like the townsfolk of Innsmouth.

George That may be, but it would seem a self-evident truth, that to get an education is to get a job. Even though the economy is ever-more unstable, there's nothing more to education. There's no place to realise what it means to be fully human. There's no real freedom to create something new – and I don't mean only works of art, literature or film. This instability, this self-created, manufactured image of instability in the global network of capital is a clever veil built from appearances, manipulated and propagated by the system itself. We are wired to this through the body.

John I agree. It is becoming hopeless. It makes your Westhampton education even more difficult to bring to life. Crisis makes meaningful change nearly impossible. Crises paralyse.

Scene 4

George It's ironic. That politics, economics and society really are the best and there's no more work to be done – except for some tinkering at the edges. Everyone who knows about these things agrees. There's no need for alternatives. But I don't believe it. The experts say philosophy is dead. If they could hear us they would probably say Westhampton is wasting its time in trying to establish an alternative form of education. In time, it'll get eaten up once it's wired into the global network of capital.

John But why should we allow that to happen?

George Because the experts tell us Westhampton is promising false dreams – it's wasting all of our time. History may not be quite at an end, but the great political and social experiments of the past are conclusively destructive and ultimately totalitarian. Capitalism, like our modern parliamentary democracies, is the most workable and successful compromise human beings have invented.

John But do we believe they are right?

George If they are, let's stop wasting our time. Let's all become piecemeal social engineers and policy directors for governments – or managers of institutions. Let's get jobs in the current system and do our best to engineer change from within.

John We've tried that and it fails. It is rubbish. There is something rotten at the heart of the system.

They stopped talking, as if waiting for more, but John didn't continue. The mood shifted, and in the silence and uncertainty it gave life, an awkwardness grew.

Scene 5

And then, with some anger and frustration in his voice, John continued:

John But that is exactly the question. The political scientists, economic specialists, sociologists and perhaps even psychologists – all with their pseudo-scientific methodologies – say there is no need for this kind of imaginative talk. Who are we to argue with them? We're only…

George Amateurs?

John Wasn't Socrates basically an amateur? Do we stop? Are we indulging something which is out-of-date, perhaps a little old-fashioned? Aren't we better off conceding the creation of a just society to the bureaucrats? Those who know that bringing in a market logic will fix everything. Perhaps we should step back and let the professors of education, the experts, the professionals with their impressive list of publications and their experience of debate in rarefied halls of academia do the thinking and imagining. We have to decide.

George Well, you and I may not be up to it. We have no intrinsic authority. We're not experts on these matters. Neither are we particularly wise.

John That's what most people would probably say.

George But I'll be damned if I don't give it a try. Even if I am ordinary.

The students cheered and clapped.

Scene 6

John So Westhampton is developing a different kind of education. What kind of education? Will its education restore our human life? Will it destroy this subservience to the systems we create? Will Westhampton educate us so we don't become emotionally sentimental or intellectually immature? Will its education restore what Emerson calls our human essence? Please assure me: Westhampton won't become a new-age institution.

George Oh God, no!

John There's something cynical in how capitalism exploits genuine spiritual yearning and turns us into consumers of metaphysical goods. We read the latest writings of some guru. We follow the words of someone who has achieved spiritual enlightenment and peace. We pay for their wisdom. We join a new cult. We want to efface our pain and suffering but we only end up blocking it by inflating our egos and self-images. The spiritual tourist, the quintessential capitalist in religious and spiritual mode. Simply sample different traditions and practices for a small fee then return to the banality and stupidity of our material lives.

George I understand what you're saying.

John So does it come down to the teacher or the syllabus?

George Both. The question for Westhampton is this: what form of education can we create that links these inner questions with the outward questions of social, political and economic organisation? Certainly not an obsession with a skills-based education – core skills, key skills or functional skills rubbish. If we don't engage the human sense of wonder then everything is lost.

John Doesn't everything come from that profound sense of mystery, awe and wonder?

They paused.

Scene 7

George Some of the ideas of Westhampton University are already out there inevitably co-opted by capitalism. You hear a lot about innovation, creativity and imagination. They agree education needs to make things, to construct realities in order to discover knowledge – to synthesise disparate facts and events into meaningful wholes rather than take everything apart all the time. But the core purpose of Westhampton education is not to sustain current human systems in politics, economics and society, but to radically invent new ones, concrete ones. Ones that have justice at their heart and not money or power or ego.

John I wonder what a degree programme would look like that did that.

George Can you imagine how much enjoyment students would get in using their imagination to invent worlds? –

John – A bit like science fiction?

George Yes, but not as entertainment. Something more political.

One of the students got up, nodded to everyone, pointed to his watch and, quietly gathering his notes, slipped away. It was getting late.

Scene 8

John So how do we construct realities without building on false assumptions? How do we proceed without repeating past errors? How do we avoid the same ideologies, attitudes and thoughts that have led us to the edge of the abyss?

George I'm not sure we can. There is always a risk in any adventure, as Whitehead said.

John Surely we need to make assumptions explicit to clear a starting point? The place where the error was originally formed or where the assumption was made. Of course we can't get rid of every assumption but at least we can dig up all those woven into our habits and traditions.

George Yes, I agree. We still need some form of critical theory. In a rush to be imaginative we cannot abandon it. It has to have a place at the roundtable. For a genuinely new path we have a lot of critical work to do.

John Inescapably so.

George But if that's all we do – critical theory – then we'll end up lost in some waiting room, going through our arguments and fine-tuning our analyses while the main event is always deferred. It might be brilliant, but its initiates will enclose themselves upon this brilliance.

John Funny you say that. Look at where we are. Almost fifty years since the radical thinkers of the 60s and the world is more capitalist, not less. The political left has almost completely been dismantled. Academia is more career driven, not less. Education has lost its way in the crowd and noise. Why? Because we've almost exclusively relied on critical theory in one form or another to do our thinking. But having left it to its own devices, it has begun to move like a trapped snake, constrained by the complexity of its own self-referential activity. And now it has begun to consume itself. Meanwhile life, everyday working life for the rest of us, has become a nightmare from which we cannot wake. With critical theory, where is the pressure to set out a constructive path, open a door to a new set of possibilities? Generate an alternative? Even though it is haunted by these ghost-like alternatives at the periphery of its gaze, they're very rarely taken up.

George Westhampton uses some elements of critical theory to clear the ground, to bring us to a starting point. That's always there. It then develops methods to pursue concrete, substantial alternatives. And this work, as opposed to purely critical work, needs lots of different people, bringing their expertise to help imagine and think through meaningful alternatives. This working together is why the university is organised differently.

Scene 9

John I really hope this will work. It could be an amazing world if it did.

George suddenly stopped and began looking through some notes in his lap.

George I've had a thought. I know it's late and we should stop. I was thinking back to what we were saying about critical theory, and I found myself saying that if we only criticise current situations, then do we not run the risk of fixing them, or making them permanent? Has critical theory – especially because it hasn't offered an alternative – actually sustained the status quo?

John What do you mean?

George Critical theory needs something to criticise. If that's all you do, all you are familiar with, then surely you don't want your academic career to end if someone says critical theory isn't enough?

John I'm sure that's unfair, most people would be happy if the world became more just and less fragmented.

George That's not my point. I'm not sure that capitalism is really suffering from critical theory. I think it can pretty much take anything that attacks it. I think it can consume its enemies.

John But we can say the same about your Westhampton education, can't we? Capitalism can make it all one great game. Invent a world, a politics, an economics.

George Possibly. But what if someone actually came up with an alternative so powerful that capitalism couldn't' re-absorb it? Like an alien that destroys the host. A seed planted in the capitalist body, feeding off it, consuming its parasitic energy and life, to then burst out through the ribcage as a fully formed monster.

John That sounds violent.

George It's getting late. I'm tired. Can we continue this tomorrow? Same place, about 4-ish?

The students agreed. Everyone got up, and in small groups went off in different directions. I remained seated for a few minutes, looking out over the late evening scene through the window. A moment later I quietly slipped out, noting the time and date that all would gather.

Act Three

Scene 1

When I returned to the library lobby George and John had not arrived. Some students were sitting around reading, writing up some notes. I took up my window seat and waited. I drifted off and found myself lost in situations that might unfold over the next few days. I sat up. Still no John or George. The students told me they were not waiting. I got up quickly and headed into the library, with its labyrinthine hexagonal spaces and endless Escher-like folding levels. I turned left at every third corner, up every other set of circular stairs – my earlier life, studying here every day, had given me a sense of familiarity in this vast library. After a confusing 20 minutes or so I finally turned right. And there they were.

It seems that after I had left, an argument had broken out between the librarians and John and George. The library entrance was not the place to conduct this type of conversation. The university had proper places. John and George had agreed to sneak in and find a quiet corner of the library and continue the conversation, close to the ancient philosophy shelves.

The same small crowd had gathered with a few unfamiliar faces. I quickly placed myself out of sight by sitting behind several others on the floor. John and George were at the circular writing table. I leant back against Marsilio Ficino's translations and commentaries on Plato, the volumes that helped spark the European Renaissance.

The conversation was already in full swing.

George I've decided that the University of Westhampton will be made up of a number of different and relatively autonomous Colleges – much like the University of London in the 1980s.

John Is it run like a business?

George A business? The moment an educational organisation is run like a commercial business with students as customers, a fundamental human relationship gets corrupted.

John Why should business corrupt education? Why shouldn't it make it more efficient, more focused and better at doing its job?

George You really think that?

John Not only me. If you are going to present an alternative, then tell me why so many educational institutions across the globe are being run as private businesses? They're not all doing a bad job.

George It depends what the job is.

John What is the problem here? Why shouldn't students be customers demanding a good quality education? Why shouldn't institutions have to compete with each other so that the people who want to gain qualifications get the best value for money?

George The problem is a lot deeper, and we have to go a bit slower if we're going to see it. Firstly, is education basically about individuals? I go to a college for my own benefit, get a qualification so I can get a better a job. Is that the point of education?

John Creating a more educated population to take up jobs in the economy. That's why governments fund it. If we didn't have qualified and trained populations we couldn't run the economy.

George Anything else?

John Nothing else that matters to most.

George Well, let's ask a slightly different question: what if this image of education, as a service industry, treating students as customers, looks like common sense but is actually directly contributing towards the increasing racism in many countries, the proliferation of conflicts between nations, ideologies and absolutes and the breakdown and instability of our human world? What if the seemingly sensible image, of servicing the economy and making people more employable, is a degenerate form of education?

John Why should it be destructive? Isn't that a privileged, elitist perspective? That we should all stop this worrying about jobs and earning a wage and, instead, do high literature or philosophy?

George Elitist, you say? The current system is riddled and corrupted with elitism, a global moneyed elitism. You can buy an education. You can opt out of the state system, leave it to those who can't pay. Let them worry if their local schools have the resources and teachers who are free. With money you can access networks. And those networks can get you better jobs. Even if your child has no talent. Meanwhile, for the rest of us, the state system is in permanent crisis. Everyone tells us it is constantly failing. Just how can it resist being constantly rewired to serve the flow of capital? Even if the economy is unstable. Funding mechanisms, private ownership, parents being forced to pay for their children's education, becoming slaves to working life. Don't pretend that the world is built on justice and fairness. Money is rewiring education. What we have is a capitalist mode of educational production and consumption.

John Capitalist education?

George Yes, something like that. But why should we carry on assuming that the economic, social or political systems are a simple given? Why should education be so passive towards them? Why so servile? I was watching the news the other day and listening to how experts and economists were talking about education. For them it has become nothing more than a part of the economy. It is discussed in terms of money – money going into the education system, and economic functioning units coming out.

George Didn't Pink Floyd sing about education once?

John It's the principle, isn't it? The obsessive auditing, the policing of standards, the rigidity of syllabuses. The completely administered society. These measures of education are moving us further and further away from anything that matters. Too heavily regulated by the very systems it needs to challenge. But how do we break the spell?

George I think it's time to challenge some assumptions, time to argue that without a radical or revolutionary education, humanity will make the next century more violent and destructive than the previous. This capitalist education is a corrupted form of education that actively breeds violence, alienation and discontent into the fabric of the world.

John That sounds so pessimistic – surely it will change, surely it will see its own shortcomings and support a new age which is post-capitalist?

George Come on John, stop fantasising. We need substantial alternatives, not political tinkering at the edges, not more time spent improving the outputs for the economy. We need to shake the system up.

John But do you have even one alternative that is not ideologically mired in past violence?

George Only one for the moment. One for how a new form of education might nurture and grow alternatives once it has recovered from its passivity to current social, political and economic formations.

John One will do. That will get us started. Yes. That's why you need to continue with Westhampton University. But I can hear something in your voice. Why are you so angry?

They paused.

George Am I? I didn't notice.

John Perhaps you need to hold on to your anger? We know that this reverence for the corporate capitalist system is entirely destructive for education. Unless we speak up and force our voice into those spaces in the mainstream, unless we re-appropriate the public debates being colonised by capitalism – unless we present an alternative, we are lost.

George People have to live in these systems. Don't be so harsh. Perhaps I am angry but I repress it, perhaps this critical talk stirs something inside me. But it doesn't feel like it moves us forward. It feels like a rage that traps me where I am, feeling powerless and overwhelmed.

John But we need to be stirred up by this. It matters.

Scene 2

George I'd like to continue. One of the colleges is at the edge of Westhampton, in a small suburb of Westhampton, Nothingham. Nothingham specialises in a range of vocational subjects, applied sciences and so on. Another is University College, or UCW, which lies at the centre of Westhampton itself. And there we have the heart of the Westhampton education. The image I have is of a wheel with a centre and spokes radiating out to the edge. It doesn't do traditional research as we know it. It is a world-creating institution.

There was a pause as several students scribbled down the image.

John Now that you've started with these details, we should also start discussing how Westhampton is run, and at some point, how it financially supports itself?

George At some point we must, you're right. Not just yet. We're not ready. Let's try and get a clear picture of the way its education is organised first.

George was standing, leaning up against a bookshelf holding a copy of Rousseau's Emile. He closed the book and sat. The students who were making notes, leafing through some of the books while they listened stopped and turned towards John and George.

George I'd like to start with a simple question. Perhaps this is the question we should have started with: What actually is education, what is it for?

John That is important but I have another question – a question about prejudices. I worry we might end up reinforcing them. In the way you have set up the two colleges, Nothingham and UCW. This image of a liberal education and a separate vocational education. This split – the former at UCW at the centre of Westhampton, the latter out in the suburbs at Nothingham College. At the heart of Westhampton education is this pure generative, creative stuff, and at the edge, in the suburbs is practical stuff. And Nothingham specialises in the practical stuff: plumbing, hairdressing, car mechanics, catering and so on.

George I don't really like this liberal versus vocational split at all.

John Then why place the vocational institution at the periphery of Westhampton, in a suburb called Nothingham?

George paused and studied the room, with its bookshelves reaching up and up, the small gathering of students, mostly now sitting on the floor, leaning against the shelving.

George I see what you are saying. But let me clarify – the application of knowledge, the practical skills are not marginal and unimportant. But they are not at the heart of a revolutionary education.

John My point exactly. That's a problem.

George Can you stop interrupting and let me finish? You've expressed what lots of current educational thinkers want – get rid of all that liberal, humanising education, reading classics and reciting poetry, push it off the centre ground and put skills at the heart of things. That's what the economists and businesses want. That's what our education should do. Put Nothingham College at the centre of Westhampton and UCW in the quiet and leafy suburbs, where it will do no harm.

John It's not a political issue.

George But that's exactly the problem – it is a political issue. Those in power, the beneficiaries of this capitalist system, understand what's at stake, they understand the real power of a liberal human education. They know that some of the best and most valued courses across the globe, from Harvard to Oxford have a liberal human education at their heart. But it's only for an elite, the moneyed classes. Those who will come to occupy positions of power. For those who can't pay for it but want it, it is blocked. How? Clever PR. Get the right message out, and the majority will treat a liberal education with disdain. A few cleverly placed images will do the trick.

John What images?

George You know the ones. That this type of human education is pointless and idle. Privilege protects privilege. Let me ask you: why pay for an education that everyone can get for free? Stop them from getting it for free. Make the rest of the population do functional stuff, practical stuff. Because they can't do all that heavy thinking stuff, they don't have the background, the culture or privilege. It's not in their DNA. A liberal human education is nothing more than a lot of idle wasters sitting around, posing abstract meaningless questions about things. That type of popular image. That's how you stop people engaging in it.

John Really that simple?

George Yes.

Scene 3

John Then what is Westhampton University proposing?

George A human education for all – one that places the best of that elite, privileged education into every school, college and university. That's how education can subvert the system.

John A subversive force from within the system itself? What the few have to pay for everyone gets for free?

George A way of renewing the system, not through outward violence or ideology but inwardly through exposing human beings from all backgrounds to the simple reality that our political, social and economic formations are not natural and inevitable, but human-made, constructed. Educate them to imagine new worlds, using science, art and philosophy, excluding no one but not limiting the world to a one-dimensional ideology. Let that education nurture and grow. Let's see what it produces.

John The possibility of moving out of this 'end of history' talk, this obsession with technocratic solutions to everything?

George Can you imagine what might happen?

John That's like a science fiction novel made real.

George picked a book from the shelf and turned it over in his hands.

George Do you see my point? If vocational or practical education lies at the heart of the Westhampton education system then it becomes the same as our current systems – equipped only to serve what is already 'out there'. It justifies its own existence on the premise that the economic, political and social worlds are given. It has to accept them. Begin to question that, then Cassius will step forward and kill Caesar.

John I see. You are proposing that Westhampton University actually has the seeds of a revolution at its heart?

George That's my instinct. Vocational education is a form of necessary servitude to the status quo. It can be dignified, honest and fulfilling, but it is premised on a given world. A true revolutionary human education creates an individual that can imagine new worlds.

John Imagine new worlds?

John sat back.

George My point is, I am not reinforcing old prejudices – far from it. I see something radical at Westhampton University. It begins with the classical liberal human education but it's got a more radical take on it. Like its take on Plato.

George paused. Several students started to clap but were silenced by the majority. John smiled.

John Good. I'm sick of the same-old same-old, the rehash of the same debates, the lack of imagination, the lack of depth and breadth. The creeping and insidious infection of market logic taking up a parasitic life at the heart of education.

George I agree. Our age is exhausted. The last embers of its past glories are fading. A new type of secular prophet is emerging – one we should worry about: a techno-fantasist of the worst kind – dreaming anti-human realities for the future of education, wishing humanity was more like a cybernetic dream, re-wired to function better. They want a better world. Their ambition is to emulate the perfection of the computer.

John Less fantasist, more fascist. Like the Italian Futurists a century ago? In love with the machine.

George straightened up.

George Yes, exactly.

A hush fell over the proceedings. George looked away. John stared up at the shelves. The students moved and quietly began talking to each other. After a few minutes some got up and left, assuming the conversation had finished. John began to gather up his notes and George stood.

Scene 4

John It's true that when Plato set up the Academy people were already learning through being apprenticed to a master in a particular trade – medicine, carpentry and, I would guess, hairdressing. What were you hinting at earlier? That Westhampton University doesn't need to teach vocational subjects? Is that a job for apprenticeships?

They gathered up their remaining notes and left the library space, followed by some students and myself, quietly at the back. We made our way through labyrinthine corridors, up spiral staircases and across floors, all the while John and George continued to talk.

George That question doesn't interest me. There's a broader question we're missing: what is the role of the human sciences in all of this?

John What do you mean?

George Do we actually have a human science worthy of that name? A human science that serves the need of understanding who or what we are? A human science that does not reduce these questions to some branch of the natural sciences. As if knowing brain processes reveals something of our human essence. I'm not against natural scientific education. I simply want to know why we don't have a meaningful human science. What we call a human science is nothing more than a branch of the natural sciences. Its methods and models are of the natural sciences, including its number-based mathematics, extensions of what is used in the natural sciences. They might occasionally engage philosophy and literature, but generally this version of a human science diminishes us in trying to understand us, it reduces us, fractures us, turns our skin inside-out, studies the brain and loses the mind, picks apart the rhythms of the heart and loses our soul. It thinks that providing evolutionary extrapolations from the biological sciences or structural circuit diagrams of the brain explains us. It assures us that meaning is an illusion, an epiphe-nomena. It tells us, if there is no meaning then religion is a fraud. Why have faith in what is ultimately meaningless?

John So do we actually have a human science worthy of that name?

George No. A human science cannot be a variation on a theme of the natural sciences. A variation on a theme with human as the object of study. Traces of a real human science are hidden away in the folds of philosophy, literature, religion and the political sciences. That's where we have to look.

John What you want doesn't really exist.

George I know. Meanwhile the economic fundamentalism of capitalism saturates our education system, burning everything with a corrosive cynicism. Look at what it does. We put our children through it. Look at how they emerge from it.

They paused at an intersection between five library galleries.

Scene 5

George I am told we have ethics, political science, psychology, sociology, anthropology, archaeology and philosophy, religion and literature. But I say none of them hang together. So what, why should they? Why should they indeed. I'll tell you. Each of these disciplines touches something of what it means to be a human being. But they don't hang together, and their fragmentation forces artificial gaps into our lives. And because we have no unifying, coherent or significant human science, we have no unifying idea of what it is to be a human being. We are creatures that are artificially split along invisible lines.

John But why do we need a unifying human science? Why can't we use what we currently have?

George A human science is not about prediction, nor causality, nor mechanical explanation, nor a reduction to the electrical and biochemical processes of the body, nor the history of development of the species we call evolution. A human science fails us when it can do nothing more than stick to the methods and mathematics of the natural sciences and treat us as another object alongside every other one.

John But why should that be a problem?

George Because the success of the natural sciences is the success of the predictive technologies of certain models and mathematics. When we turn these predictive technologies on us we confuse the nature of the object. How can the subject that created these models and mathematics – designed to generate predictive models as evidence of truth – be completely circumscribed by them? Something goes awry. We are the beings that have created predictive technologies, elevated them to the status of a science, but we are also the beings that have created art, literature, philosophy and religion to serve other purposes.

John Is that why a human science cannot be a natural science with a different type of object?

George Yes. We have to start from a dual perspective and build principles that recognise our intrinsic creativity and imagination. The clue lies in the plurality of our religions, in the variety of our deepest philosophical speculations, in our greatest fictions and artistic productions. The philosophical, political and ethical questions about how we should live need to be grounded on principles that do not reduce the human to a sophisticated algorithm or calculating machine. We might be constrained and conditioned by evolutionary forces but how meaning operates in our lives cannot be reduced to these or any other constraints or conditions. Heidegger sensed it but left too much out – ethics, religion and politics. A human science needs to arrive at its own principles that do justice to the fullness of our humanity, and our deepest experiences.

John Why should a human science be so different?

George Because what we say about a human being frames how we human beings actually exist. A human science is not just descriptive or explanatory. It is generative, not just predictive. It doesn't simply observe and test – it generates realities and we, as subjects, situate ourselves in those realities. How can that not be significant? If we allow our current fragmented human sciences to persist, then economic fundamentalism will end up dominating everything.

John Why call any of this a science? Sounds more like a mixture of art and philosophy to me.

They had arrived by the library entrance. The sofas were packed with students revising for their end of term exams.

George I think it is a mixture. But why leave the word science out of this? To call it an applied art or applied philosophy simply dismisses what Westhampton is trying to do. We need to reclaim the word science from the methods and mathematics of our predictive technologies, from the natural sciences. We need to define a human science that is not reductive. If we reject the importance of a real human science what will be left? The human broken up into different categories? We break up the human at this level and we create the conditions for conflict at all levels. So another century of warfare, this time the totalitarianism we fight will be religious and not secular. Why should you and I leave it alone? I want a human science that uses the imagination and couples it with reason and logic, not to create a new description of the human, but to generate new possibilities of what it means to be human, to find new ways of living. That's what I mean when I talk about a human science.

John But science suggests something systematic. What you're doing sounds creative, not systematic.

George It doesn't. It's just a cliché that it must be either systematic or creative. It can be both. It sounds too ambitious but is it really? We are after all the species that made rockets and put a man on the moon. Let me tell you how Westhampton University has tackled this. All its major specialists came together over a period of 27 years. Some worked with religion, mystical thought and a range of esoteric schools in both east and west. They took core mystical, hermetic and esoteric ideas from within all religions, boiled them, distilled them, dried them into a powder and then turned a tiny bit of this powder into ink. They used this ink to forge a new mathematical art. In parallel, some took this powder and added clay to mould conceptual machines. These conceptual machines were then applied to philosophical texts. Slowly, after years of repeated application – in subtle variations – they began to extract a number of hidden seeds. They then planted these seeds in the soil of the imagination and nurtured the plants. Once fully matured they extracted the flowers which were crushed, dried and chopped up. Water was added, a paste was formed, then rolled and flattened into paper, given time to dry. It was upon this surface that a new art of 'pataphysics, ontology and ethics was written. One final group worked on drama, literature and myths, and another on the contemporary roots of psychology. During these 27 years these specialists worked in secret, maintaining their day jobs to pay for their living, mortgages and families. None of them relinquished the belief they could create what was needed. They worked on primitive categories which bridged semiotics and hermeneutics, core formulations which lived at the heart of language, science and everyday life. The miracle was that this mathematical art – this conceptual art written in a mathematical notation – was actually built. To teach and apply it they formulated its grammar, the rules of combination and permutation and interpretative strategies. And so they formed Westhampton University as the home of this new art of world-creation. A place where new alternatives could be generated from these principles and concepts derived from years of study and patient work.

John Behind this description you give lies something real, doesn't it?

George Yes, there is something real here. One breakthrough for the specialists at Westhampton, something they stumbled across during all this work was the way meaning emerged into the world, how it operated and worked – both in human life, with its social, political and economic dimensions, and across the whole natural order. One of the core courses at Westhampton is all about meaning, its grammar, its structures and patterns of flow, its linkage to time. If Plato, the ancient aristocrat, is a key inspiration we should also mention Spinoza, the outcast Jew, earning his money as a lens grinder whilst quietly developing an image of God, the soul and the world that was the heresy of all heresies.

George paused.

John Really? You expect me to believe any of that?

George Yes. Really. Try to imagine it, or something like it and you will see what Westhampton can offer the whole education system.

John You're insane. You've made up one spectacular fantasy, a very appealing one but a fantasy nevertheless.

George It's only fantasy because you can't imagine there is something real in what I've described.

John No, it is fantasy because, amongst other problems with it, you are basically challenging not just the natural sciences but pretty much all branches of knowledge. What you've described makes no use of the natural sciences. It seems they don't hold the keys to developing a human science. This talk of a mathematical-art, the sense that the human sciences are deeper and more important than the natural sciences – is that Westhampton University marketing? Just how do they intend to overturn 300 years of successful natural science? And what is all this talk of conceptual art?

George I know it sounds impossible. But I have seen it. It is the one truth behind the fiction of Westhampton.

John But it is impossible. What would such a thing look like?

How would it work? How could anything like this actually overcome the gap between the core of our inward spiritual experiences and the outward realities of our social, political and economic worlds? I can't see it. Don't get angry. I just can't.

George Because you have never had to think or imagine it. We're all the same. The way we compartmentalise these different bits of life and thought and experience. This work at the heart of Westhampton puts an extraordinary image at the heart of its education, something that is not a theology or some obscure esoteric fancy which dissolves into nothingness when you get up close. Out there, in our so-called real world, if we carry on as we are we will lose a lot more than an education system. The natural sciences will simply carry on strengthening capitalism. Technology – including all the destructive powers it unleashes – with its merciless machinery, will wreak havoc upon the face of the planet in the name of some corrupted ideology, some fanatical, reductive image of humanity. This ideology doesn't just come from the religious terrorists. That's lazy. It also grows inside the corridors of power of our political systems, hiding in open sight, with those market fundamentalists.

There was a pause, as if John was digesting what had just been said.

John There's nothing like a Westhampton education around. That's what I mean. Something built on a rigorous intellectual foundation, one that has the power to counter the corruption of our ethics and politics and growing leech-like terrorism, one that shifts the axis of science to the human and derives the categories of a natural science from there. It's difficult to see. A bit like seeing the death of capitalism and its violent offspring.

George I agree. But don't you want our human world to change? Don't you sense that we are heading in the wrong direction –

capitalism has infiltrated and duped our scientific institutions. They have formed an unholy alliance. It's not just out there, fighting in desert wars, but in here, inside our institutions.

John Duped science? Have they?

George Both believe numbers and number systems are fundamentally real, more real than concrete and particular human life. It sounds crazy but the market, with its number logic, its computerised algorithms – it determines the economic welfare of our everyday lives and our social and political institutions.

John So why so much instability?

George Instability? That's it, isn't it? That's an image projected out of the system itself. Is it real or manipulated, or a function of the algorithms, the machinery of this system running on automatic? Are you and I taking too much for granted, trusting just a little too much? Just think about it before you condemn Westhampton. Is my very fear and anxiety paralysing me, trapping me in in this system? How can I be so sure these instabilities, generated from the operations of this system, won't spiral downward into a violent chaos? Is that what I want? What if these instabilities are signs of a systemic malfunction? Are we risking global catastrophe? So let me ask the question: can you and I risk not finding alternatives to it?

John Look, there's no getting away from this – what you are proposing is impossible.

George I disagree. The possibility of generating alternative forms of economic, social and political life has to be given time to breathe and grow. There is a profoundly human force in you and I, which is borne out of a yearning for meaning and justice that can be woken up. This Westhampton education, based on a human science – linking the arts, literature, religion, politics, psychology, sociology and so on –, all relating coherently to the natural sciences is too important to dismiss. What was once called mystical must become accessible to all people, not as some supernatural myth or fantasy, but as a reality of everyday life, as a basic experience of being alive. Surely you believe that?

John I do, but I wonder whether you have dreamt up something that can't be realised.

George Every child should have access to an education that helps them fully realise their humanity and their connectedness to everything. Otherwise we condemn them and us.

John paused.

John Shall we sit for a few minutes?

George Okay.

Scene 6

They sat back in the same sofas in the library entrance hall. The students joined them. I found a chair near the back.

John What you're saying seems more like a 'pataphysics' – a science of imaginary solutions – than a traditional metaphysics or ontology. It doesn't fall into the traditional categories at all. It sounds so different from anything I know. That's what I can't get my head around. I'm not sure a 'pataphysics' has this kind of power.

George People like René Daumal would probably disagree.

John The academic world seems content not to challenge things, like the way departments are split up. Most wouldn't know how to cope in a world in which the separations of arts and sciences, pure and applied, technology and humanity – you know, this broken up, specialised world – wasn't in place. I doubt they would be receptive to you.

George Ordinary people might be.

John Are you sure? Most people work for a living and struggle to eke out a quality of life. They split their lives up into private and public, work and entertainment and escape. Where do they have time to listen to this or be challenged or stimulated by it?

George Yes, but that is what makes this work more urgent and important. You and I have to make these concepts work in their imagination if we are to persuade anyone that it is worthwhile.

John You don't think your thoughts are new?

George No, I don't. The seeds of these thoughts are over 2000 years old.

John You mean Plato?

George Further back, but Plato's books capture those earlier trends. He shows that thinking and imagining are not isolated activities in our heads but occur in social settings. That is important. Through social gatherings he experimented and explored with all kinds of thoughts – including the thought that there were patterns or forms at a deeper level of reality than our senses. But the secret of his philosophical thought wasn't a philosophy of forms, but the use of the social and political imagination.

John In the Republic?

George In everything he wrote.

Scene 7

John sighed.

John But people need jobs.

George I've never denied it.

John So here's a thought: what about political, social or economic engineers? To generate models for society, politics and economics? Is that a possibility?

George Not sure I would call them engineers.

John But at Westhampton University people could train to do this, couldn't they?

George I'm not sure we can reduce it to a job. We need to start earlier. We need to educate our children to look at the political, social and economic forms as constructions, things that are built to serve life, not the other way round. A bit like teaching children to imagine utopias. To create their own and then compare them to what we actually have. To put imagination into education. Make it part of life. Not what it has become under capitalism – an escape from life.

John But we already have this in our elite institutions. In political science departments.

George Partly, we do. That's why I am reluctant to talk about it as a form of social, political or economic engineering. How do you fit religion into this engineering concept? I don't think you can. Issues to do with this human science are not simply a repeat of the natural sciences. I think it's very different. For a start it is interdisciplinary – it cuts across different departments in a typical university. Westhampton is built on an interdisciplinary model.

John I'm not sure I see why you are using the word science if you're against the word engineering.

George Okay, let me put it like this. Let's not talk about political, social or economic engineering – as you say that's already in the system. Let's talk about spiritual engineering.

John What?

George Sounds ridiculous. So why does it sound ridiculous? Partly because modern engineering has grown up as an applied part of the natural sciences. The whole thing relies on the framework, mathematics and concepts of the world given by the natural sciences.

John Yes, but you've talked about a mathematics for this human science and you've been happy to talk about science – or your concept of a human one. Why shouldn't we imagine engineers?

George Because it suggests you can become an engineer of the human spirit without undergoing any change yourself – other than learning how to do the mathematics and solve problems. It's the wrong image.

John But you want people to learn about this science?

George Yes, but the process of learning and exploring opens up imaginative possibilities. It doesn't require an engineer to solve the problems. Unless we use the image of a spiritual engineer.

John But that sounds ludicrous.

George It is more accurate. Westhampton University has a human science and is using it to teach this art of world-creation – and all of this is systematic and structured, based on a mathematics of its own. For them spiritual engineering might be the right image. Not only do you apply this science outwardly but also inwardly. It sounds mad because our system completely discards spiritual and religious matters as private, and aside from religious education classes or one's own faith based activity, it never figures much in the system. That's probably why it sounds mad. Perhaps the day when a 'spiritual engineer', or something like it sounds obvious and sensible is the day some subtle change has occurred in our thinking. But I wouldn't want to use a job definition as a measure of success.

John It's funny. Now that you've got me started I am curious.

George About what?

John What kind of society would employ a spiritual engineer? What kind of world would that be? It reminds me a bit of a novel by Herman Hesse.

Scene 8

George Well, are we making any progress?

John Other than realising the extent to which the current heart of our education system is becoming more inhuman. The way technology is constantly driving change, that the economic world is unstable, jobs aren't guaranteed any more, there are forces beyond our control – globalisation, capitalism, terrorism. It's leading to a kind of restless and anxiety-ridden paralysis – a sense of dread. This world is becoming more and more fragmented. Meaning is breaking up. And it needs continuity, it needs a different movement.

John paused.

John There seems to be a contradiction in our nature. On the one hand we seem entirely limited by the social, political and economic forms we inhabit. Our understanding, our basic categories of existence emerge within these forms. They have no eternal status. We seem to be purely historical beings. There are some societies in which it is impossible to be a good person without being destroyed. Like Nazi Germany. But there's a problem. I have heard some say that even in Nazi Germany people had a sense that something was wrong. That their social and political forms had become so deeply corrupted and warped. Even if most didn't fight it. But where would such a sense come from? Personally, I'm not sure I believe they did.

George It suggests that our nature is partly rooted in something deeper. Something that gives us an orientation that might transcend the boundaries of the social and political forms we inhabit. Could it be that our human nature, our soul, is rooted deeply in the flow of life and this root reaches below any particular social, political or economic reality?

John Then what goes wrong?

George The inner and outer are not separate. From birth, these social, political or economic realities operate on our souls, on our human nature. They can sever our rootedness to this deeper source in life. Or distort what flows into us.

John In the way Rousseau sensed some forms of civilised life damaged our natural state?

George Possibly. Just because we are formed within corrupted social and political realities, does it follow we are completely corrupted by them? Or does something in us remain outside of being corrupted? Something real, that just can't be digested by any social, political or economic reality? A remainder?

John You mean is there hope?

George Without hope, would we feel pain and anxiety in our everyday lives? Pandora's Box all over again.

John We can't recover this by escaping into some mystical ground or running off to some ashram and to gain enlightenment.

George No, of course we can't. I'm not saying that. We might be rooted in something deeper, but these social, political and economic realities are hardwired into our lives.

They paused.

George We should have a break. I am getting tired.

George stood. There was a moment of hesitation. The small group disbanded with a mixed air of melancholy and hope. I left quietly and returned to the library, to Plato, to read more of his ancient conversations. I found myself, some hours later, falling asleep wondering why conversation was so natural to human life yet so few writers had written them.

Act Four

Scene 1

The day started badly. After a fitful and restless night with work anxieties creeping into dreams I struggled to enter the day. In a state of anxious indifference – if such a thing is possible – I spent a day doing what I was told, being spoken rudely to by people in charge and feeling tired and demotivated throughout. A weight hung over me, a sense of wasting something precious that I had been given. After a few final phone calls I left work and made my way to the library.

Different students had joined the group. More sofas had been dragged over. The peaceful spot by the window, the small upright chair was still there, as if it had been reserved for me. Without saying anything I quietly sat and waited. John and George were in the middle of a conversation and one of them was scanning some notes.

John Why is our political system and those who rise to positions of power in it so mediocre and shallow?

George Because our politicians seem to have all become economic fundamentalists and emptied politics of its ethical responsibilities? I don't know.

John In the 1960s and perhaps even the 1970s, there was an explosion of gurus and spiritual leaders and guides springing up all over the place. They came down from mountains, like Zarathustra, uttering gnomic parables and implementing obscurely designed spiritual practices. Some operated outside of any traditional religious or political framework. Nearly all of them claimed they could restore our humanity. There are still a lot of them around. Perhaps they answer a genuine need that our mainstream politics fails to…

George A gnawing sense of meaninglessness?

John Yes. An ugly leech-like parasite seems to have crept into the soul of our politics. Most people don't link spiritual issues with politics. Politics is the management of the economy – the mantra of the economic fundamentalist. Spiritual matters operate at the individual level only. That's the neoliberal consensus. But most people are wrong. Ask Spinoza. They are linked, profoundly so. And because they are linked – and we don't see it – we don't see that this new age movement, born in the 60s, has become nothing more than a self-serving industry, feeding off the yearning of the human spirit. It can never work.

George Why?

John If our basic systems of politics and economics remain as they are, serving capitalism and turning a human being into a 'functioning economic unit, then no degree of spirituality consumed or smoked or fed intravenously into the human body will recover the sense of meaning.

George I would agree with that.

Scene 2

John picked up some of his notes and read.

John For the creed of the economic fundamentalist, politics is a priesthood designed to serve structures and systems of numbers over and above the human being.

George Hang on! Structures and systems of numbers? What are you talking about?

John Haven't you noticed that reality is glued together by structures and systems in which the only objects of value are numbers? Look at it carefully. It's not just in politics and economics. Numbers lie at the basis of everything. They are the ground upon which we build our homes, the fuel that supports the flow of goods and foods into our lives, the basis of our identities in our working lives. That's why the economic fundamentalist worships these structures and systems of numbers. Soon the air we breathe, the love we feel and the God we listen to will be drawn into these structures and systems.

George Surely there's more to it than this? People are also in these systems. Surely that's got to count?

John Count for what? How do people affect any of this? Our political leaders legislate more structures and systems to support the flow. Listen to their conversations – debt, borrowing, interest rates, GDP, savings – it's conquered everything. This economic fundamentalism. And in this coming century, in the growing digital world, we will probably end up finding reality only within computerised systems – the actual presence of some physical token will disappear. Our systems may not become conscious – like those science fiction fantasies –, but they will become the bureaucracy of capitalism as it solidifies into electronic concrete.

Scene 3

John So tell me, how do we fight it through education?

George We have to counter this dominance of numbers as the basic object of mathematics. It helps to see different movements in mathematics, those that are more concerned about form, structure and pattern. These begin to move us in a different direction. They can make us see the possibility of a mathematics deeper than one we have.

John How?

George To begin with, Westhampton treats the idea that mathematics is just about systems of numbers or sets as secondary and derivative. They say these ideas feed capitalist ontology, the proliferation of algorithms that wire everything into digital fantasies, consuming and digesting everything in their path, reducing the world to electrical flow through computerised networks. The brain and body becoming wired into these cybernetic pathways largely through screens, constantly pouring out images, movement and entertainment. What capitalist ontology leaves out is marginalised and then excluded – labelled as a nothing, a failure, the drop out, useless. The official line – generated by the economic fundamentalists sacrificing everything at the altar of capitalism – is that if it can't be assimilated into the cybernetic network it is superfluous, a waste, a remainder.

John To be thrown out into the wasteland beyond the city gates.

George But it is where meaning hides, escaping the brutalisation of the capitalist machinery, with its desire to wire everything into its mathematical ontology. It is in this excess that our humanity veils itself, avoiding capture like a criminal accused of crimes that have no name. A capitalist dystopia. Away from the bright surfaces and loud voices of functioning economic units hardwired into their networks. A cybernetic nightmare.

John And how do you counter the presence of this mathematical ontology, this mechanisation and corruption of number systems?

George You need an alternative mathematics.

Scene 4

John stopped and stared at George.

John In the meantime?

George In the meantime we erode our humanity. We open up the parasitic consumptive to the life-blood flowing into us. We shut out of politics anything that might challenge this ontology, this view that the world is a system of numbers. We grow older, our rebellious spirit gets ensnared through financial worries. Without noticing, when we thought we were discussing things that might change the world, we find ourselves talking about property, our way of life and our work – as if there's nothing else. And quietly the parasite kills off something in us metamorphosing us, in turn, into parasites. With an important position, one that makes a difference – its real, I've got status and people respect me. The system has disappeared and I don't see it anymore. To subvert it from within you have to shine a bright light into those places that are neither unconscious nor hidden, places where your complacency sits, places where the wasteland grows. To do this there's some pain. You have to rewire your soul, sever yourself from the capitalist matrix. We think we have power. We think we have democracy. But everything is manipulated, corrupted. And we become agents of corruption, especially when we take it all for granted and switch off. The nation-state legislates to support corporations. The solitary human being is rendered more and more powerless to resist. The age of the romantic hero or rebel is over, except in our entertainment industries, where it acts in a way we can't, where it wins in a battle we dare not even enter. Like a bright costumed ghost standing before us, satisfying the desire for justice for the cost of a cinema ticket. The age of the corporation is upon us.

John What then is democratic leadership?

George Something we've lost. In its uncorrupted state a form of governance that isn't reliant on personalities. A form of governance that allows reason and humanity to speak.

John So what do we have?

George What we have is something that simulates democracy. You join a party, conform to the party line and diminish your own political consciousness. The group becomes the unit of action. But this group needs a leader. In a single step, what was once freely formed, dynamic and fluid generates an autocrat from within itself. The autocrat hides inside a mask of democracy. They get a seat in parliament and then they wreak havoc on education, the health system and so on – justifying their behaviour because they were voted into place. Oh, and they understand the economy. Our simulated democracy is corrupting. It corrupts the moment the person fuses with the position. That is exactly what the system demands – the removal of any excess and the complete identification between myself and the role I occupy.

John Why is this inevitable?

George It isn't. When you occupy a role in some organisation there is a gap. How you occupy this role is not a given. You have to think and negotiate your relationship to this role. You have to think across the gap. But the truth is that the gap is essential. You need to be constantly aware of it. Don't fall into the trap that your own personhood has some intrinsic linkage to the role.

John But isn't that how it begins to corrupt?

George I short-circuit the gap. It closes. I am fused with it. I make decisions but I don't give reasons. To question me is to question the role, and that makes us all vulnerable, all of us who hang off this role. So no one questions. Or, only questions within accepted parameters. This fusion of personhood and role makes me untouchable and outside democratic accountability.

John Or it makes me completely vulnerable.

George Yes, if you are an ordinary worker this fusion makes you profoundly weak and puts you into a permanent state of anxiety – your performance is the measure of not just what you do, but who you are.

They fell into silence. The students all seemed to be writing.

John So our democracy hides an autocracy at its heart? A parliamentary autocracy?

George But there's more. Look at the career politicians, public relations executives and professional business people that fill the corridors of power in our democratic systems. Look at the absence of a basic political consciousness in the education system. Is someone trying to keep us all from noticing? Except, ironically, for the elite institutions. And they're the ones recruiting young men and women into posts in our governments.

A student quietly got up, nodding to all, glanced at his watch and scurried away. He looked nervous.

John We like to think capitalism is a western creation – and it is – but it's an illusion to think it is intrinsically democratic. Look at the success of capitalism in communist China. Plato described tyranny as a corrupted form of government. He was right. But it is not a person who tyrannises us. It is a system, an impersonal system – riddled with chaotic fluctuations, laying waste to vast tracts of the world population. And yet it still manages to serve an elite wealthy minority.

George How cleverly it veils itself from scrutiny by generating its own anti-capitalist propaganda.

Scene 5

John Let's get back to Westhampton. How does it guarantee it hires leaders with integrity? Not only that but how does it stop corruption growing from within the leadership of Westhampton?

George Familiar story this. They began by trying to put policies and strategies in place. They then realised this needed a kind of internal police force to enforce it. They publicly announced the creation of a justice committee to which this police force answered. Monthly meetings, highly prestigious, honorariums dispensed, titles added to staff badges for those who joined this internal police force. But after some time, power and corruption shifted from the leaders to this police force. Suddenly the first step in an infinite regress had begun. The committee set up another police force, but concealed this one to stop staff being bribed and paying for favours. It didn't work. This hidden police force became more powerful and its presence became destructive. The committee began to lose credibility as more and more secret meetings and dealings became the order of the day. Paranoia crept in. The core work of Westhampton, however noble and idealistic was being compromised by outside deals. Money came flooding in and the work of the institution began to serve rich patrons. When one of the managers, one with integrity and well respected, became the focus of the secret police and was not only destroyed through it but had to resign, the university board realised this system had failed dramatically. It was premised on deferring responsibility on to either policies or policing.

John So did they find a solution?

George They're in the middle of an experiment. They founded an alternative ontology from this mathematical-art and made its teaching a fundamental part of their activities.

John An alternative ontology? Why does that help?

George It's all very-well running an educational institution and it's all very-well assuming your job is to administer and guide the institution, but if you have no personal connection to what lies at its heart, then your presence will be marginal and your ability to advance the institution will, in the end, become self-advancement. It has to mean something to you personally. Their idea was simple. Publish the basic principles and charter which support an image of the cosmos and humanity as a single whole. A charter that includes religion – both in theological and mystical dimensions. And – perhaps, more importantly – they include various forms of secularism and atheism. This charter spells out how important this is for the leadership at Westhampton University.

John You do realise this is such an unfamiliar demand for a university to make of its leadership? It sounds like a seminary where conduct is linked to the ontological and ethical values of its traditions.

George Crucially their tradition is secular.

Scene 6

John Something you said made me think of how people get promoted into positions of power. It is blighted by nepotism. I personally blame our infected politics – it now infects everything, including education. Our ideals are wilting under the scorching sun and we are letting them die through our inattention. And it's going to get worse. Every successive government tries to break the spirit of education so it can remake it in its own image. Freedom is more and more regulated and performance managed. It has to be earned and justified through blood and pain. Is it value for money? Can our economic overlords use it? Those fools are killing us.

Scene 7

George You might argue that serving the overlords is not the same as being a slave to them.

John God, is there no hope for us? If we continue to run our education institutions in this way, how do we expect to change the world, how do we expect to truly educate the human and not serve those masters and tyrants that talk, like robotic imbeciles, of students as customers, who demand research must always be useful and economically beneficial and who are frozen in empty postures and hollow gestures, constantly looking out for the new elite, the growing economic aristocracy: CEOs, media moguls and corporate autocrats.

George If Westhampton and its colleges, Nothingham and UCW are not to fall into these same traps, then we need to break the spell of the autocrat and that of nepotism.

John Who should get into leadership positions at Westhampton

University? How do you prevent corruption? If democracy is vulnerable, what chance do we have of protecting our fledgling Westhampton?

They both paused.

Scene 8

George This may not be appropriate, but if you remember, Plato talked about philosopher-kings. He tried to imagine a kind of person, who underwent an education that turned him or her into someone who could not be corrupted by power.

John Yes, but wasn't this a kind of aristocratic, fascistic leader?

George How is that fascistic? He believed that a kind of philosophic discipline – not simply attending university and getting a PhD –, but actually going through a rigorous training was the way to create leaders who cannot be corrupted. In his view – and he had Socrates partially in mind – the philosopher is intrinsically not interested in wealth, power or status.

John So you're suggesting that's what we have to invent? An education that will make a person incorruptible? I think that whole approach is flawed. How can you stop human nature being corrupted?

George Perhaps an education which develops the critical and sceptical side with an ethical and imaginative side? The former without the latter gives you cold and callous rationalists – the latter without the former gives you escapists and sentimentalists. I mean, where do people of integrity come from? Are they born like that or nurtured? And what education will nurture integrity? Isn't human nature fallible, prone to error?

John I would avoid the trap of thinking of a sort of monastic or ascetic discipline is what is needed. The Taliban unequivocally prove that religious monks are the most susceptible to corruption – a kind of religious totalitarian. Years of seemingly ascetic training, and in a flash, their egos explode with self-righteous violence. Personally I think we can't have Plato's philosopher-king or philosopher-queen, and we're not going for the unworldly or ascetic, and I'd add another proviso – an autocrat is also prone to corruption.

George Then who can lead Westhampton University who has integrity and will not be corrupted?

John It doesn't leave us with much. Is it hopeless?

Scene 9

George No, it can't be. Perhaps we can approach this question in a different way. Let's ask another question: where do we recruit from? Get someone from the business world? A popular trend in education.

John Oh God, no.

George Why not?

John Are you serious? If you have no personal experience of engaging with philosophical, political or intellectual matters, how are you going to know how to lead it? If you've never given over part of your life to creating or discovering something, then what meaning would it have to you? Surely it will be an alien activity? How could someone in that position actually lead Westhampton? How could someone in that position support a revolutionary art of world-creation?

George You need someone who has undertaken some original work, who has devoted their life to the pursuit of knowledge or understanding. We'll end up with an ascetic again – someone so worldly inexperienced they wouldn't be able to cope. Or some well-heeled career academic who will ample proof to support their work.

John And if this type of person cannot be found? Or prefers to work on something rather than lead an educational institution? I'm not sure any of this will work. Perhaps the problem is of thinking a single person is the solution – making all authority rest on that person is flawed.

George I'm not sure. Perhaps we need to institute a different idea of reason? If reason is chained to the natural sciences, then it will fail us. It has too many blind spots. If reason is the glimpse of heaven that Mephistopheles describes in Goethe's Faust, then perhaps it might work. Perhaps we've attacked one image of reason – this narrow, scientific image – and forgotten that there are others. When Kant talks about the courage to use your own reason, he doesn't mean doing a scientific experiment or gathering data – he is closer to Goethe than to us. When Descartes says reason – or common sense as he called it – is evenly distributed amongst all humans, he was rejecting the privilege of authority, not trying to institute another authority we must be subservient to. Neither of them thought, as some popularisers of modern science think, that reason on its own is enough, that it needs nothing else and its products are the only ones that count. Don't forget, Kant said reason is limited – something we would be foolish to ignore.

Scene 10

John But we're still in the age of Stalin.

George Stalin? What do you mean?

John The fantasy of the absolute ruler. I think enlightenment faith in reason collapsed in the twentieth century and in its ruin gave us Hitler, Stalin and hundreds of absolute rulers – a century of the worst kind of fantasists. We're in danger of repeating the same mistakes, but instead of secular clothing it's in religious clothing. Perhaps it's going to be much worse.

George You're right. The collapse in the belief of a rational society violently failed last century – even in France, a country that gave birth to the dreams of the enlightenment, a country now as susceptible to its own form of state fundamentalism – its secular anti-religious absolutism. Its revolutionary roots have not managed to halt the rise of the right, of anti-immigration, fear of the other, subservience to capitalism. And remember modern France was founded on a revolution that was partially inspired by Rousseau.

John Is this entirely hopeless? We want something that is supportive of integrity, intellectual freedom and a kind of spiritual ambition – to make life better without falling into simplistic political formulas. Let's find a robust model of leadership and administration at Westhampton University.

George Yes. Let's.

John A system that prevents the identification and collapse of the person with the position of power.

George It might help if all our leaders had something else to do – research, teach, or some creative productive activity that allowed them to prevent this fusion of person and leadership role. It might be right to look at a form of governance in which everyone who occupies a role of authority has not only a personal life outside of their work, but are all productively involved in something else going on at Westhampton. Something to counter-balance their leadership and provide an alternative source of meaning.

John Didn't the ancient Athenians have a similar idea? Draw everyone into the legislature and government on a rotating basis, make everyone take a part in the management of society? Actually, it was just men, wasn't it?

George Even though it's a good idea, it ends up failing.

John Yes, sadly true. The Athenians suffered from those who came into government to serve their own interests, fed by teachers and sophists who taught them how to manipulate. No system can be foolproof. We have the same problem. There is too much desire for power in our human world, too much desire to control the flow of capital, to wire the capitalist network in your favour. The philosopher or thinker who questions and who might expose all of this is much maligned, ridiculed and dismissed. So they'll challenge you – come on, where's the answer? What's the alternative? It doesn't matter if I don't think or read about these things, it doesn't matter that I spend all my free time wired into entertainment. I can still have an opinion. You still have to persuade me. Give it to me in a soundbite or I can't deal with it. Give me a solution that I can rip apart. Expose your thinking. Can you handle it?

George I cannot satisfy them. Why these trusting, weary and hard-working, easily manipulated, easily persuaded ordinary people become an enemy to change I don't know. Why do they pin their trust on some figure, ideally one with charisma, but in the end, a puppet will do. And then our democracy is a fiefdom with its own inner-circle of capitalist stooges. And everyone knows it's corrupt. But that doesn't stop them. Hypocrites. Disavowing their subservience, all the while maintaining the status quo. Little worlds of power. That's what we have.

George That's not a good point to end on.

John Sorry. I'm tired. The world is catching up on me. Things are not good at work. Let's have a break.

They all agreed to meet up at the Cafe and take the conversation further.

Act Five

Scene 1

The next afternoon the Cafe was crowded and noisy when I arrived. The tall windows looking out across the park and square opened up the space to the sunset glow, shifting reds, oranges and deep pinks. In the far corner, in one of the raised alcoves, were John and George chatting and scribbling on sheets of paper surrounded by the same group of students. I slipped over and sat at the edge of the group so I could listen. No one noticed me.

As if an angry thought was bubbling away George spoke aggressively and quickly:

George Can I start?

John Go ahead.

George I've noticed how our collective health is collapsing under the weight of servility to the given economic realities. We're becoming more and more medicated in our daily lives. It's not the pleasure of Huxley's soma but the antidepressants of an industrialised world that we consume. The problems only keep on growing, adding layer upon layer of stupidity and half-thoughts with fads and endless systemic anxiety. In the meantime you and I are in danger of reducing education to a service industry, a call centre. I think it's already infecting universities and colleges. You contact your local college in order to obtain a service from them. Can we really say the current system – with its endless government auditing, it's targets, it's performance measures, it's funding models and so on – is actually making things better? Education isn't free. This fractured market-logic guarantees its perpetual servitude. I fear what might happen in this century. Why doesn't education serve us instead of serving our economic systems?

He stopped and looked down, looking at some notes.

Scene 2

John You mean a more brutal question: why are we so weak and passive in the face of the new holy order, the new priesthood of money, the God that hides and delivers justice through the magical powers of the market? Where our children, teachers and students should be experiencing mystery, wonder and awe, there is only anxiety, fear and worry. Will Westhampton University break this disenchantment? Can idealism succeed in our current climate?

George I've been thinking about this a lot. Simply adding in creativity is not an answer, even though lots of expert education-alists talk about it. It's another version of the same disen-chantment, and simply another way of serving the same master.

John Well you posed the problem. How can any educational institution actually be free? How will Westhampton resist these political and economic pressures?

George I don't know if it can. I think we need to be bold and courageous, to side with Westhampton and what it is attempting – even if it is futile.

John I agree.

They smiled at each other.

George Westhampton has written a manifesto for education. A manifesto of the future of the human species and its home, Earth.

John I like that.

George It begins by saying that a core purpose of education is not to serve pre-existing social, political or economic realities, but to be free of them. Westhampton administration wants the university to become a place where new human possibilities are generated and explored. The aim is to change the world, but not according to a formula or equation. This is not a return to a simple 'ism'.

John Those students who come to Nothingham or UCW – what do they study?

George Okay, I need a cup of tea before tackling that.

The conversation paused, drinks were ordered, and slowly people drifted off, answered messages on phones and laptops, then returned to the conversation.

Scene 3

George To make sense of the courses at Westhampton I have to unpick some current practices and beliefs.

John Okay.

George Education currently splits and fragments knowledge, from pure to applied, from the natural to the human sciences, from science to art and so on. Today, much of education is about selecting which path you want to take, which career you want to pursue.

John But what's wrong with that?

George It's entirely wrong. What if the separation between the natural and human sciences were inverted? And then a newly self-grounded human science was built on a mathematics of its own? What if the core of our education also started there? What if Westhampton were right to found a human science on principles that apply to the natural sciences, but are not derived from them? Principles which have distilled philosophical thought, religious experience and the myths and fictions we generate? It would be like an event of being, would it not? Everything would shift. The natural sciences would retain their dignity, but no longer occupy the throne of reason. It would have to be relinquished to a human science. You would be able to study the natural sciences in relation to the way our under-standing of the natural world frames our understanding of the constraints in which we live. You would be able to study a human science that required a grasp of Gogol, as much as it required a grasp of the meaning of calculus. So then, here's a thought: what if the question of how we live, how we organise our human realities – all these systems we construct and then pretend they are given to us – what if a new method was developed at the heart of Westhampton, one that critically challenged politics, social and economic practices by generating alternatives?

John An interdisciplinary method?

George This method would be generative. Through the imagi-nation you would formulate skeletal artworks, artworks built from a new mathematical notation. These skeletal forms would be images of metaphysical wiring, of souls. They would portray structures of the flow of meaning into the world. And these skeletal structures would provide the basis of generating alter-native social, political or economic realities. Keep on formulating different skeletal artworks and new alternatives would emerge.

John Until?

George Until one worked. Perhaps a trillion alternatives would need to be generated and explored before one emerged that would feed off the current system and give birth to something so radically different, one that would smash our cave-like existence and force us into the open air under the light of the sun.

John Tell me more about this method.

George We need an image. We have lots of images of making things – from physical artifacts to pieces of music and poetry. What this human science has is a method for making skeletal artworks, symbolic structures that portray a flow of meaning.

John What do you mean? How can you put meaning together?

George No, you can't construct meaning through this method. The structures you construct are flow-patterns of meaning. Meaning flows through things, events, situations and movement.

John Meaning of what?

George The meaning of life. It isn't a thing that can be held. It flows through the events of your daily life. That would be one type of meaning. Then there is the meaning of our actions.

John What? Now you are being silly. Are you saying that meaning cannot be captured? Is it not a form or structure or object? Can it not be pinned down? What are you saying?

George It is flow through the world. The meaning of anything lies in the way this flow passes through it.

John Wait a minute! This human science, which is supposedly built into Westhampton education, is an education which you claim has a revolutionary core, an art of world-creation? And it is related to constructing meaning? I don't see how it would work. The meaning of things is so personal and subjective. How can you turn that into a science?

George Meaning flows through the subject as it does through the object. This method doesn't tell you what something means. The way we interact, the flow of communication, the way a disavowal in some situation changes the flow of interactions in other situations. This is how the world moves. Both subject and object are wired into this flow. Meaning has an order, a grammar, a language and vocabulary – and there is an order to the way meaning flows through the world, not only how we respond to it but how it works. This gives you the basic starting point to building alternative social and political forms.

John When you say 'works', I find that difficult – the thought that meaning can be boiled down to some kind of machine.

George I didn't say machine.

John Alright then – like a machine? Input all the relevant elements and it will output a meaning?

George Well, meaning is more like electricity flowing. It pours through our machines and computer systems. There is no formulae for the meaning of things because meaning is not the word, the object, the symbol, the act, the thing. If it were, then some clever person would have put a meaning-machine together and it would help us all live, albeit by some formulae or algorithm. Our lives could be lived according to a fixed pattern. And we'd all be happy. Ignorance is bliss. Right?

John People have tried.

George Yes, but part of the reason it has failed is that the process of constructing a meaning changes your situation, the very activity of participating in this science and education changes you and the world. It's not like doing a bit of engineering mathematics. You go to work, do some calculations and then get your results and go home, much as you were when you started. This science actually involves you and challenges you. That's what makes a Westhampton different.

John I need to think about this. It opens up so many questions.

George Shall we break and come back to it?

John Let's have a break. I've got some chores to do before the evening is out, and then I will try and sleep and come back to this fresh. I have to admit, something in what you've said has struck a chord with me. Perhaps this revolutionary method of world-creation can really work.

George didn't reply, he simply nodded and got up. A hush fell over the group as they quietly moved off and left. It felt like the conversation had been interrupted.

Act Six

Scene 1

A few days had passed and I found myself back in the library, sitting by the window. News was out that John and George were busy working on courses and details of Westhampton University.

The library was quiet and the image of the two of them trying out a new idea, breaking new ground made me smile.

I got up and was about to leave and return to my own work when I noticed one of the students that had listened and been there making her way into the library. I waved to her and asked her where she was going. John and George had got together in one of the library spaces to chat about something, and news had got out. She was on her way. I asked if I could join her.

After several minutes we climbed a spiral staircase to find John and George sitting on sofas under the sun dome near the top of the library. I fell back and found a seat so I could remain unobserved.

John Last night I bumped into Freddy Faust and we went for a drink and chat. I told him about our conversation and Westhampton University. He got really excited. I did explain that we'd barely got started. He wanted to join us.

George Interesting. We might still get others involved. And this needs to be a movement if it is going to work. Some kind of collective imaginative experiment. A real conversation amongst lots of groups – sending each other their thoughts, conversational transcripts, building up images of alternate realities, not beholden to state nor any ideology past or present.

John It was interesting how our new conversation moved. Freddy thought about what you wanted – it's a real big deal, he thinks.

George Which bit?

John All of it. This human science, this mathematics of a human science, this education, this art of world-creation – this university that shields its students to give them the freedom to imagine and think alternatives, to uncover a real revolutionary way of being. He loved all of it. He did say funding is another question. If you crack that, then you have the birth of a trillion revolutions. And the real possibility of a peaceful global civilisation.

George Coming from Freddy, that's really positive. For me, he always hides behind a cynical mask.

John Because he hates the way things are going in education. He hates all these in-built structural injustices.

George Yes, that's a good way of putting it – structural injustices. *They paused.*

John He told me about the place he used to work in. He told me about something that happened to him, which brought his career as a teacher in a university to a dramatic end. He thinks it captures how corrupt things have gotten. And cynical in its corruption. And you know what they say about cynics?

George No.

John They use their cynicism to pretend they are above the corruption. They're too clever. But it's a trick, a trick of self-disavowal. Their cynicism allows corruption to persist. It's actually how they hold it in place.

George What do you mean?

John It's a form of modern quietism, a form of acceptance made in bad faith.

George It's also a sign of moral decay. This inability to take responsibility for your own actions, the reluctance to exercise your own judgement and reasoning, the reverence for a certain type of authority. It's a backward step.

They stopped.

Scene 2

John A few years ago, Freddy taught philosophy for a little while in a university college. They had to cover a topic on legitimate political protest. The students were extremely bored and detached. They just didn't get into it. Freddy had a problem. What to do to engage them? He decided on something more interactive. They made up an issue: the closure of the art, literature and philosophy departments. Students were given the justification, the corporate justification: the future of prosperity and the economy was given entirely to engineering and science – with a twist. With the culture of humanities and arts about to be marginalised, and the degree programmes about to be closed, in a cynical move, to compensate those who love the humanities the university introduced some kind of entrepreneurial stuff. It drove the students into a rage. Once all this was fired up Freddy gathered a few colleagues and some willing students, and they collectively put on a mock protest at the main gates of the university college. They made up banners, wrote a manifesto, dressed up as 60s hippies and stood at the gates during most lunch breaks – in between their proper classes, sometimes at the end of the day. It was entertaining and a lot of fun, perhaps too much. Students loved it. The student union got involved, other lecturers got involved, and the college newspaper ran articles on it. It was partly a parody, but a sense of injustice had been fired up, people felt they had something to protest about. Remarkably, some of the lecturers used this as a way of introducing the students to Pataphysics, Dada and the Oulipo.

George But?

John But it all went horribly wrong. A group of enthusiastic politics students really got into it. They dressed up as Argentine anarchists. They made really colourful banners, including some hilarious pictures of Borges as a kind of a Guru. Around this time, a few weeks into the whole thing, it was getting so popular that the local radio station decided to see what all the fuss was about. During a particularly warm lunch break, with the radio team interviewing staff and these colourful students making a noise with music breaking out in the protest line – the college president drove past. He was coming back from a business awards event in London in a chauffeur driven car with partially blackened windows. The students say they didn't know who it was. Some obviously did.

George What did they do?

John They got carried away and began a broad and aggressive anti-capitalist rant aimed at the president's car. The driver, a part time lecturer working extra hours to make a living – and a close friend of Freddy's – was told to slow down so the President's PA could photograph everyone.

George Oh dear.

John Yes, indeed. News got around the College that the president was furious – "How dare they behave like that – how dare they encourage this type of behaviour. This is unacceptable." The students were unimpressed. They began a secret campaign – using social media – about corporate leadership: leaders with no imagination, full of airs and graces, a sort of assumed self-importance, modelled on royalty and aristocracy. The senior management team, a bunch of leeches, both feeding the president's grand delusions and feeding off the scraps thrown in their direction, in a self-righteous mood kept on pouring more petrol on the situation. A student wrote a brilliant critique. I have it somewhere – oh, here it is: "It's a power regime that is entirely mutually parasitic. The actual autocrat is fundamentally a leech, a creature that is entirely dependent on other leeches that it feeds. The leech disavows its dependencies – it needs to mask these in order for this system of power to exist and sustain itself. Those who are subservient disavow their relative power over the autocrat in order for the power structure to exist. This is all part of the unconscious mechanism that keeps power in place. Education cannot have this type of leader ruling the system. This leech-like autocracy. Yet another form of corrupted government." When this was printed on leaflets, the leadership at this university college completely and utterly went into a rage. Someone was responsible, someone had to be punished. This inner circle, the leadership team, sitting with the university college president took this offence as a case of professional misconduct. It's a classic move by those in power – change the terms so their interpretation is not an interpretation. They called an emergency leadership team meeting – and the disease began to spread. Lots of angry leaders came to express their views through the following days. With all the threats flying around, including the actual closure of the humanities department – now actually being considered – the mock protest took on a real-life dimension. Staff panicked – all have mortgages to pay – and began to disappear and put their heads down. By then Freddy realised his cards were marked – already his department head had begun an investigation into his behaviour. Had he brought the university into disrepute? As if this wasn't bad enough, the local radio then passed the story on to a national paper, and the regional television station wanted a story. When news of the television station wanting the story spread to the president, he wanted to see them. Bizarre as it may sound, he went down and argued in favour of the experiment. In fact, he made out that the university encouraged this type of political simulation. It was what our society and politics needed. The television people left with some great quotes. He then instigated disciplinary action against staff involved for breaking internal procedures. If such a mock-protest was to be carried out, there were processes that needed to be followed.

George Invoking a set of rules and procedures when you feel like it. Almost impossible to fight because the transgression of rules, the tacit leniency for those on the inside, are carefully hidden, whilst those on the outside aren't. To challenge this you end up challenging the supreme figurehead of the rotting leadership team. It's all highly charged with ego.

John The students carried on protesting. They were not going to let this new sense of democracy and protest and its importance in history be shut down. The president convened an emergency meeting. The senior management team simply accepted his terms – the offences were catalogued because the personage of the president was offended. To disagree would mean challenging too much. And that would put you out of the inner-circle. Unopposed, the President argued that this mock protest could have damaged the reputation of the university. They were careful how they said it, so it was minuted properly. They agreed dismissal for the ring leaders was the best way forward. After the meeting, one of the members of the leadership team, filled with righteous indignation, foolishly went down to the humanities' staff room and told them that they would be dismissed. It was sheer pettiness and vindictiveness, and out of earshot of cameras, students and so on, so it could easily be denied. Freddy says he remembers it vividly. It was one of those unreal moments when the world seems to lose its balance and you feel yourself falling. It was like suddenly getting vertigo. Here he was trying to do something for education, stimulate political engagement in the subject, and suddenly he was facing dismissal.

George How does he feel about it now?

John That is something he cannot forgive. This sense of being a pawn in a petty power play. In retrospect, it's interesting that this episode signalled the imminent failure of the university college. The huge disconnect between its education and its management just became too damaging. Freddy, as you can imagine, fought back. With the news media on the doorstep this became a national news story for one day. That was his moment of fame. But it passed, it faded away as terrorist threats and immigration crept back into the news. For a brief moment the news media captured an ideological battle between education and business. Until, of course, its own complicity with capitalism quietly undercut its objectivity. The president was protected for a long time. Lots of his team blocked the critics, until it began to come out that no one really liked this detached, self-serving president. The leadership team were utterly, morally and intellectually bankrupt – dodgy international deals with questionable ethics and so on. Finally they fell. Years after Freddy had moved on.

John paused.

George It's a poor man's Gogol tale, lacking charm and wit. So that's what happens to autocratic governance. It gives too much power to an individual. Vanity and personal reputation become the central concern for the leadership – not the education.

John Ironically, Freddy said this university college was so servile to business and the economy that it was in the process of closing down the history and classics faculty for that very reason. This only emerged after this event.

They stopped.

George There are very few real people of integrity, and even those with some sense of it lack imagination and courage.

John Did Plato believe that his philosopher had integrity.

George Yes.

John You know your concept of the art of world-creation, as we've called it? Could this education turn out imaginative and intellectually powerful leaders?

George Yes. And that is what Westhampton needs. But it needs a freedom that simply is not possible if we remain servile to the economic fundamentalists.

John Yes – that is a root problem.

George stretched.

George Let's have a break. Half an hour? Get some food?

Everyone nodded. One of the students had written lots of notes during the story about Freddy. As he moved off with a friend, one of them suggested writing a play, fictionalising the story. They all began chatting about how they could make it work.
    I sat and waited.

Scene 2

An hour had passed before some of the students returned and sat, reading books. I squeezed myself closer to the window. After another ten minutes or so John and George came in from the library with books under their arms discussing something. It was something about Plato's Cave. They stopped, sat and turned to the group, scanned the familiar faces and then continued. They passed their gaze towards me but luckily didn't recognise me.

They smiled at the students and sat.

John Who do you have in charge of Westhampton University?

George Those who aspire to intellectual and imaginative freedom, who are not constrained by political affiliations or obligations to interested parties, who can think and value thought, who believe in the power of reason and the human intelligence and who have no desire to serve an ego, or become self-serving autocrats. They are not compromised by personal ambition or vanity. They prefer to gather those with critical human intelligence and imagination and are entirely against the cult of personality. They have a sense of serving something higher, and I don't mean something religious. The leadership are entirely secular in their conduct, even though they might have personal religious convictions of their own.

They stopped and let their words fall into the silence.

John But aren't these people the ones always under threat from those who control the flow of money? Isn't real power in the hands of those who control how the university is funded?

George Perhaps. Perhaps the job of leadership is to argue and make sure the funding serves a true education, one that has a moral or ethical core – a Socratic core. Just imagine if we had a Socrates today.

John He wouldn't fit into any department.

George And that is an unpleasant truth. The figure who stands at the root of the kind of education we have been talking about just wouldn't have anywhere to go. The current university system would exclude him. That's a symptom of why we need Westhampton to be something radically different. I spoke to Jacques Dériva last night about this conversation.

John I presume he had something to say?

George He agreed that a leader in education has to be one with intellectual and imaginative power. He said if Westhampton University is to succeed it must be, at heart, interdisciplinary and must include not only social, political and economic realities but legal ones as well.

John He agrees with the premise then?

George Like us, he agrees too many leaders in education are simply managing its impotence.

They paused.

John My worry is that, even Plato's dream of a philosopher-king would fail. His ideal was the aristocrat. That was the basis of his philosopher-king or queen. But, for me, there is no ideal type or ideal constitution that will serve all humanity. For Westhampton to succeed it has to prevent tyranny, power elites, vested interests and subservience to the economy infecting its leadership. And that won't be easy.

A silence fell over the group.

The conversation had reached an abrupt end. John and George exchanged a few quiet words and slowly everyone disbanded.

I sat and waited for all to leave, listening to the excited conversations from many of the students. Outside it was night. Tomorrow I had to get back to work and to my own problems.

Act Seven

Scene 1

When I returned to the library some weeks later, one of the librarians approached me and quietly explained that the small group I had been sitting with was across the road at the Musée d'Art. I thanked her and left the library, crossed the road and passed between the grey buildings. The small university art gallery was by the main entrance. I walked cautiously, again hoping not to be seen. The group was sitting around a Kandinsky.

John What about art and painting and music? Where do they fit into the education at Westhampton?

George Art is at the heart of its education. It connects back to what we were discussing about meaning. The university has a very sophisticated take on it. They say that a physical or sensory artwork is a complex sign-object, a complex signifier. What this artwork means, what it signifies, comes into life in the social imagination. In traditional beliefs you engage the artwork by looking at a painting or listening to a piece of music or reading a book or watching a film. Each artwork exists in some sensory form. At Westhampton University they have developed an artwork that only exists in the social imagination. The physical sign-object is an ontological skeleton of this artwork. The flesh is entirely generated imaginatively and conceptually.

John Sounds a bit like conceptual art.

George It is. It is an art that takes conceptual art to a new level. They call it a post-conceptual art to situate it in the relevant history. It is built through contemplation and discussion of these ontological skeletons. These ontological skeletal forms are generated from a mathematical language, a mathematical language that founds an idea of a human science. The question is: what is the ontological skeleton actually made of? Do you remember what we talked about before? The ontological skeletal forms are structures for the flow of meaning. This art is all about meaning.

John This is what you were getting at before?

George paused.

George Yes. The shapes and forms it generates – using a strict grammar – give skeletal pathways through which meaning flows. The basic vocabulary of this mathematics constitutes the basic operations and junctions in this flow. When we talked about it before, we discussed it in a different situation. In this situation Westhampton treat it as an art. They call it an ultra-conceptual art.

John An ontological skeleton, as you put it, is drawn or written-out using mathematics. This is then contemplated and discussed through thought and the imagination. It is that activity that gives rise to ultra-conceptual – or imaginative – artworks?

George Yes. The two things are connected. What is written or drawn for anyone to see is purely an ontological skeleton. It needs to be acted upon by the imagination.

Scene 2

John How does it work at Westhampton University?

George The students are taught the basic symbols, the grammar and combination of this ultra-conceptual art. Some simple ontological skeletons are generated, providing an opportunity for them to think and develop the imagination.

John Grammar? Is it a language?

George It is a bit like a language. Westhampton explores this connection through a series of language talks and discussions. These talks and discussions both explore the nature of language and how art and mathematics grow out of the limits of language and how this ultra-conceptual art combines both intense precision, while at the same time expressing a spiritual reality.

George paused.

John A spiritual reality?

George This art can represent the structure of the human soul or a whole human society, or, more deeply, the inward movement of spirit inside you, or simply structures of meaning of feeling and thought.

They paused again.

John What is a structure of meaning? That's probably the thing I need to get clear.

George Meaning flows through the world, from a root into the living branches, the life-forms that make up the Earth. A structure of meaning lays out the way this flow moves, splits, turns and passes through the world.

John paused.

John That seems straightforward. This art is linked to the spirit.

George Yes. Part of the study at Westhampton University has a strong sense of the ethical and spiritual discipline of a seminary rather than what most people understand by a university. To really enter it takes a commitment from the whole of your being. It is both intellectual, emotional and intuitive, and critically rational and imaginative. This is what Plato intended, what Pythagoras created and what the ancients and eastern thinkers all sensed – ethical matters closely bound up to spiritual matters which are closely bound up with social, political and economic matters.

John I can't imagine many people are ready to face such a thing. Isn't Westhampton University asking too much of them?

George Is it? In our age we don't need a plaster on our social wounds – tolerance won't heal us. We need insight and intelligence and imagination and the willingness to enter deeply into things that matter. Abandon all prejudice ye who enter.

John It sounds impossible. I want to go there and see it. I want to get on to one of those courses.

They paused.

Scene 3

George When I think of early humanity, I think of their endless supernatural myth making – Gods everywhere, an invisible order rich with activity and meaning. I think about the way these early humans developed primitive social practices around these supernatural beings. There was a sense of life being connected to sacred spaces – points in which the supernatural and the earthly interacted. Just imagine you could strip out the flesh from this myth-making – the complex human projections, the anthropomorphism, the realms of supernatural fantastic beings occupying realms high up in some heaven beyond the stars. Imagine you could distill this supernatural world into a set of skeletal mathematical concepts and then present these concepts combined, according to an ontological image, into skeletal artworks, which the imagination can act upon and generate worlds, societies, universes?

John That's an incredible thing to imagine.

George That's a glimpse into the revolutionary education of world-creation. It becomes a revolutionary path through art in which every skeletal artwork presents and informs us of possible social, political or ethical realities.

They paused.

John Is that how this things work. Not just analysing thoughts of others but constructing realities using the imagination? Mixing reason with artistic and imaginative freedom.

George Can you imagine what worlds we might invent and bring to life?

John And maybe one – amongst trillions – might actually work and become the basis of peaceful global human civilisation?

George That's the dream.

Scene 4

John So, is there a core skeletal artwork, a foundational ontology upon which Westhampton University has built its education? Or is that asking too much? I'm thinking back to what you were saying about all this study of philosophy, religion, the arts and literature?

George Well, Westhampton uses secular principles to found its charter. But this form of secularism is an umbrella term which includes a plural religious culture. This means, in a very unfashionable way, they are profoundly sympathetic to religion in important ways – it calls to all religious traditions to participate in its revolutionary educational methods. But that does not mean it endorses literalism or fundamentalism in religious traditions.

John But how do you get religious thought into a secular frame?

George By distilling images from religious thought that strip away the fleshly variations of various theologies and supernaturalisms. Human science built on a mathematical language can then extract the structural patterns within religious belief without collapsing them into a new theosophy or diminishing their meaning.

John But won't you alienate the atheists, nihilists and materialists if you bring in religion?

George Like the religious fundamentalists or scriptural literalists, they also occupy dead ends. They belong to a postmodern world, a world of flat-ontologies – the nothing below or above thinkers, the thinkers who get caught in complex subterfuges which deny when they affirm and affirm when they should deny. A kind of zombie apocalyptic thinking. Simply rejecting whole universes of human experience because of certain fashionable attitudes will not heal and unify human life and bring about the possibility of a peaceful global civilisation.

John What is a flat-ontology?

George The belief that life has no depth, there is nothing below or beyond the psychological, and the psychological is just a symptom of biological or neurological processes, all of which has developed through evolution. It is flat and empty – and meaningless. The idea that there is something below the material substratum or something beyond laws of nature – something that might be dynamic, ecstatic and alive – is based on an empty myth.

John The tacit belief system of capitalism?

George Here's the mistake – you don't have to agree with fundamentalism or the literalists to recognise the deep spiritual and symbolic truths contained in our religious traditions.

Scene 5

John But if we rely too heavily on the imagination, won't everything simply become fantasy? A day-dream or illusion?

George No one claims that the things of the imagination are real – in the way you and I are sitting here talking. That's not the point. But the imagination, when properly developed, accesses realms that are too subtle for thinking. Some call it an imaginal realm – a realm that lights up within us when the imagination translates these subtle levels of existence.

John So, what particular image forms the foundation stone of its educational charter?

George We start with Heraclitus and Swedenborg and an image of a ceaseless irresistible influx within and under the world we encounter. This world we see, the world in which we go about our daily business, is a reality that emerges out of this influx, this movement that cannot be stilled or captured.

John But if that were true, why does it fill me with anxiety and a feeling of a bubbling chaos underneath or within the everyday world. How does that help? In monotheistic religions there is a God underlying the world. Have you banished God?

George Wait a minute. There's more. This influx that Westhampton prefer to call an ontological influx, leads us to further questions: where does the ontological influx come from and return to? Is it really like an endless bubbling river with no end, no direction, and no source? All religions say that there is a source, a root, out of which everything arises. But this source, this root of life, existence and the cosmos, is directly inaccessible to thought – thought is too clumsy and lacks the subtlety to do anything more than approach it. That is why there are meditative, contemplative, imaginal and other spiritual disciplines. From an ordinary, everyday point of view this source is a mystery – it is what mystics experience as the root mystery of life and existence if they encounter it or approach it. It cannot be measured and captured, dissected and shared or sold or bought. Capitalism cannot get hold of it. Numbers cannot get close to it – in fact, all traditional mathematical systems fail before they get close to it. Even though they emerge from it. As Borges put it: it is the Aleph out of which the whole of existence pours and returns. Not only does everything flow out of this unknowable root, but it is also present to us at the base of our ordinary consciousness, it is the foundation of our intrinsic freedom. There are no fixed structures, forms, rules or laws that pour out of it, as many classical scholars maintain. None of our social, political or economic formations are given. They emerge at the intersection of history and this ontological influx as it flows into the world.

They paused.

John What is the influx made of?

George It is made of pure flowing meaning, constantly fresh and alive. Meaning is not a thing, but a pure movement up from this mystery at the root of life, into life itself.

John Pure meaning? Out of some infinite mysterious beyond? Isn't that classical theological and religious talk?

George This picture describes an ontological skeleton upon which different religious and secular systems put flesh. It stands prior to talk of a God or Gods – it stands before we begin to talk about supernatural forces. All these things emerge as our response to it.

John It sounds like a form of mysticism.

Several students began to write.

George Mysticism tends to veil the experience of wonder by pushing it on to a privileged, trained group of gifted humans. The experience of the mystic is ordinary and belongs to everyone. The mystery of life and its purpose is not hidden. But remember, to access it, is not to access an answer. It is to experience the wonder and the amazement of existence.

John So how does this ordinary world I experience emerge out of this influx, this river of pure meaning? Sounds wonderful but most people are stuck in fear and anxieties in daily life – isn't there an enormous gap here? The life we live seems to be enclosed, trapped, and there are only outward escapes – for which you need money or power or position.

George This living ontological influx generates from within its own flux 'seeds', temporary forms which appear and disappear. Universes grow out of these seeds.

John Seeds?

George Yes, there is no simple word for this – seed is the best I can do – it connects us to the image of growth and nature, and a living, natural meaning. Imagine the surface of the sun – the way sun flares burst out and project themselves out from the surface of the sun into the solar system. Think of this ontological influx like a sun. The solar flares are universes, worlds and life which pour out, stay for a little while, but then return to it. These forms that emerge combine to create worlds – like a forest of plants, a tapestry out of which our cosmos and the everyday world emerges. Each form, each plant, embodies meaning. The basic atom of the cosmos is closer in complexity to this plant. The cosmos, as a whole, embodies a flow of meaning. It is dynamic, unbroken and alive.

John When you say meaning do you mean a scheme, a plan?

George No, I don't. The root flow, the ontological influx as I have been calling it, is alive, it has a spiritual presence. It is organically related to everything that emerges out of it, and in turn it relates back to the infinite source, the mystery, the root of all life.

John There is no separate agent doing all the creating work?

George The cosmos emerges out of this influx, this metaphysical stream. It grows out of it, like a living plant growing out of a fertile, life-giving river. The craftsman image of a deity is a theological image that tries to flesh out this image. It wants to place ethics as something given. But ethical systems emerge with lots of history and context.

John This raises more questions than it answers.

George I know. For the moment let's push this a little bit further.

John Okay.

George Let's say that every form that emerges out of this influx embodies something of the mystery of life, that its form expresses something of the root. Therein lies the mystery in beauty and love. And a revolution without beauty or love is a birth of a monster.

George paused.

Scene 6

John Is there more?

George Everything that we encounter only subsists through this influx, this movement from the root – from this metaphysical stream. It is constantly pouring and generating the world we experience, the world of our senses. The moment the flow into you or me ceases, we return to the source of this metaphysical stream, the mystery of all things. Those questions are open.

John There is something odd you've said, but not lingered on. This influx pours into you and me?

George That's what I am saying. That is the basis upon which Westhampton University connects to the students who arrive there. This ontological flux is where it all starts. I am not talking about a secret agent buried deep within your everyday self – though some like to talk like that. I am talking about a flow of meaning which sustains the cosmos and you.

John If what you say is true, then why are so many people anxious, full of fear, full of a sense of belonging to no one and nothing, lost and floating in this everyday world, dangerously susceptible to any outward force? Why are so many of our modern human experiences like this? Doesn't the reality of our ordinary human world suggest we are cut off from any influx, that such a thing is inaccessible to us? Has something happened to us that has broken our inward experience of this influx?

George You're right. As this metaphysical stream pours into us, something deeper than our everyday thinking ought to touch us in some way. Why doesn't it? Why is the basic experience of daily life full of anxiety, insecurity and fear?

Scene 7

George Let's assume our minds constituted by this metaphysical stream. Your question of how we are full of fear and anxiety, how we conduct ourselves in such destructive ways is absolutely critical. How was the Holocaust possible if this metaphysical stream was operating? Look at the barbarity of the twentieth century? Our barbarity would contradict a cosmic dimension to our selves.

John Exactly. It raises a question: is this image you've described right? What if there is no meaning underlying the universe as we know it, no metaphysical stream? That would accord with the terror and horror of the twentieth century.

George But that simply leads us back to the same starting point. We need to challenge ourselves differently. Let's do something paradoxical, let's say with Westhampton, that this image is true. And then try and answer the question of why our lives have become so profoundly fragmented, selfish, destructive – why doesn't this flow of meaning reach our ordinary feelings and thoughts? How do we cut ourselves off from it or distort it or block it?

John Okay.

George Now we have something different. As Westhampton has found, if we talk about this we end up discussing how this influx gets blocked, distorted, refracted, scattered or lost within us. That opens up new questions. Our social, political and economic formations might be playing a deeper role in our inner lives, and if they are disjunctive, broken or fractured, then this might break up the influx into us.

Scene 8

John And what about the natural sciences? Don't they contradict all of this?

George How?

John In the modern scientific outlook it's all explained as habit and socialisation. Nothing deeper. There's nothing below or above. Yes, it's a flat reality and the natural sciences are the best access to it. We only need neuroscience and neurobiology to explain the things you were talking about – ethics, value, etc. There isn't a mind, but lots of complex brain processes – and biochemistry and genetics and – this list could go on. And there are departments out there that do political and social science and engineering. Let's for the moment say that science has all the answers or the best method, and in time will solve all our problems – perhaps develop new drugs to pacify us and make us happy. Let's assume that the political and social engineers and scientists in academic departments also believe they will solve our social and political issues. Westhampton simply needs to select the best and all is solved. What if contemporary science has all the answers, all the best explanations?

George Are you being serious?

John Yes, why not?

George If you strip away the rhetoric and politics you see that modern science only tells us that the cosmos is a complex structure that can be partially decoded by mathematics. That's it. Depending on which faction of scientists you talk to it also either tells us how meaning works or that meaning is an illusion – a logical relation or a mask on primitive biological drives and processes. Without a doubt, science increases our grasp of the complexity and richness of the world. It's true we don't need external supernatural agencies or divine purposes to make sense of a lot of the cosmos. But it's not true that the cosmos is actually only a material object that hangs in an infinite void or abyss.

They paused.

John What's your point?

George We have been spellbound by the success and power of the natural sciences to such a degree that we think it's on its way to sort everything out. But it isn't. In fact, through its technologies – including the nuclear bomb – it is likely to destroy us rather than save us.

John The argument that science gives us knowledge but it is up to us to use it wisely is surely true?

George Isn't that a cop out? Science exaggerates its own claims and status. It's done some social good in undermining obedience to blind authority – but even here it's going awry.

John Are you not bothered by these grand claims it makes?

George No, I'm not. Part of the reason I am dissatisfied is because of the world I see around me and the role of science and technology in what I see – claiming to only care about pure knowledge, but actually ethically and morally void. I would go further. Westhampton came to this thought some time ago. It inspired the development of a human science.

John What did?

George That it's not the experimental method that helped the natural sciences succeed.

John Really?

George When I see the natural sciences I see a simple assumption at work: underlying the complex variety of the natural order is something like a mathematical structure. It's the power of this structure to be captured in symbols, signs and their operations – that's the secret of the success of natural sciences.

Better minds than us are mesmerised by this. Some even concede parts of philosophy to mathematics. Even though the mathematical structure of the natural sciences is over-reliant on numbers and quantities and their variability and patterns, which is its inherent flaw – a flaw it inherited right from its starting point–, it has been spectacularly successful.

John Why 'flawed'?

George The mathematical structure of the natural sciences is too limited to serve as the foundation of a human science because its mathematics is too reductive and it subtracts too much humanity from us when studying the human. It's clear when you see the partial insights of quantitative methods in the social and political sciences, the statistical modelling techniques of political science – that it's all very flat and reductive.

John How does your Westhampton education overcome it?

George Its mathematical language maintains the dignity of what it means to be a human. It does not reduce existence to number patterns. This mathematics is also a form of art – the very way it presents itself also belongs to some of the later trends of abstract and ultra-conceptual art.

John As I've said – that's impossible.

George Some would say the human species defines itself by doing the impossible.

Scene 9

John Where were we?

George We've put flesh on an ontological skeleton and used a flowing river metaphor and an unknowable root. The cosmos grows out of this flow, and like plants, each thing exists through its roots in this river, drawing in life and movement. The cosmos is an organic living order that emerges through an influx, and every part stays in existence only insofar as it participates in this influx.

John Yes, but Westhampton's administration is sitting around a room all very impressed with this thought. Some, like me, find a lot of this impossible. How does it become a principle upon which to organise education – and how does it support this revolutionary art of world-creation?

George Because it suggests that the cosmic order is intrinsically creative and emergent, that all forms persist but have no permanence, and arise as a function of situation, history and growth. What we do and have done plays a crucial role in the forms we actually inhabit. Our social forms are not biologically determined. The idea that they are is a measure of how reductive our natural sciences become when applied to our lives.

John What you say denies the immortality of the soul and the permanence of the laws of nature? Aren't you going to offend everyone?

George Because it contradicts Christian teaching and some scientific principles?

John Yes.

George Well, it doesn't. The God of a monotheistic religion is a theological interpretation of this root. If you are an atheist you experience the mystery of life without having to buy into a theology. This picture renders those differences irrelevant. How we know this root is through what emerges out of it, much like the way we know someone through the way they respond to situations.

John But the immortal soul? The heavens and hells?

George The immortal soul – well immortality needs a whole separate conversation. Time is not uniform. The heavens and hells of theology or Swedenborg also need separate conversations. Both need a better grasp of the meaning of the imagination and what I called the imaginal.

George paused.

John Give me one implication for Westhampton.

George If all things are related, then the departmental and subject splits are actually artificial – Westhampton University is organised differently.

John How?

George Well, Westhampton University looks at how a natural ecology works, how each separate plant, animal and environment forms a part of a cohesive flowing whole. Each department has no meaning on its own. It functions within the ecology of the whole university and there is a flow of information and activity through the whole university that is fundamental to each department. The principle of intellectual freedom and the development of a new world, which involves studying the natural sciences, history, philosophy, art, religion, reading the classics – and then putting them all together to forge alternatives. The unifying action is this art of world-creation.

They paused.

John But how will Westhampton University survive in this current economic climate? Won't capitalism destroy it?

George Possibly.

John You don't seem sure.

Scene 10

George We live in dangerous times. Sticking to the accepted orthodoxies is a way to sleepwalk into destruction. It's going on out there – from fanatical, life hating ideologies couched in religious language to ultra-conservative plutocratic ones that wreak havoc with ordinary working life. We are in chaos and crisis and there's no guarantee we will come out of this. We desperately need this. We desperately need a revitalised education to create the space for us to discuss these issues.

John You make me think of the Promethean myth in Plato's dialogue, the Protagoras. Epimetheus gave everything away and left humans naked, without claws or sharp teeth. And yet humans dominate the planet. Why? Because of the capacity to learn, to be educated, to imagine and think.

George The roots of this are in ancient traditions. We need to unearth these roots and use them.

John Why not do this in an academic philosophy department?

George Because the majority of academic philosophy depart-ments are not designed in a way that allows these discussions to take root. They are technical specialisms next to linguistics or psychology – with their own vocabulary, rules of play and hierarchies. There is no sense that they are at all concerned to draw us to the roots of our consciousness and understanding and help us imagine new possibilities.

John They have conceded too much. Too much has been handed over to the new age industry and to science fiction writers or to political science departments. The education we need is scattered over too many different departments. More philosophical and creative work is probably going on in literature departments, or political science faculties. I despair at this state of affairs. In the meantime everything in our modern world is leading to greater instability and insecurity.

George That's what disturbs me.

John But doesn't your image suggest the cosmos is unstable? A flux?

George No. The cosmos emerges organically and from within its own root. It is not a building with an architect. It doesn't need a master builder. My argument is that the instability is a lie propagated by those who benefit from the state of affairs caused by fear and anxiety.

John A lie?

George paused before continuing.

George Do you see what I am trying to get at? For me to say the human world doesn't need a master makes more sense if the natural order grows organically rather than has its development masterminded by a supernatural being. This concept of a master builder carries with it all the baggage of building design, stability, foundation and so on. It's the wrong metaphor. The wrong image. Life is a flow, and living forms grow organically out of this movement.

John But then why does it all go so wrong for human beings? If this metaphysical stream is pouring through me, why do I form images of the world that contradict it? Are the images I form coming from some other source? One that is severed from this metaphysical stream or one that distorts what pours into me?

George We're too heavily wedded to the belief of a separate supernatural agent doing all the work behind the scenes. The mystery, this root of life is not an agent. If we say it is then we end up with something like a regress problem. All agency operates in a context. So we have to push further back and give this supernatural agent a context. But then what about this context? Where does it come from? We risk pushing even further back. Is there another agent that generates this context? And on it goes. Rorty said something like this about some of Plato's ideas. In trying to explain things through a supernatural agency we run the risk of getting lost in a meaningless proliferation of supernatural beings and agencies.

John Then what is this root of life?

George It is the soil out of which a plant grows. It is the infinite emptiness of Nirvana. It is the mystery one encounters when entering the Cloud of Unknowing. For Muslims and Jews it is the God that transcends any image. For Meister Eckhart it is the Godhead – not a being nor an agent. It is the condition of our existence and the way we move. Humanity can cut itself off from this root and the metaphysical river that pours out of it, it can sever its ties to this inward movement that pours into our souls, but without it the cosmos would cease to exist. And our souls are the wiring into this flow. To know it is to know the cosmos, is to study and learn about the marvels of the world as it manifests. What pours out reveals its essence. And that cannot be boiled down into any scheme.

John But we can deny it?

George We can deny it, but like the sun it will carry on shining. It is like trying to live with something covering your eyes. That is our condition.

John Has it always been there, in our consciousness?

George Yes, all conscious living beings sense this vast infinite mystery. It is not a threat or an enemy or a Lovecraftian monster, slumbering in some alternate dimension. There is something about our age, our times that seem to have blocked off our access to it, forced it to flow outwardly. But this inward blockage has resulted in sensing the cosmos as a malevolent or indifferent force. Cthulhu is born out of this denial. What violence do we do to ourselves to become socialised into this world? We sever the influx, the consciousness pouring into us of this mystery and its outpouring. Like a character in the Matrix, the contemporary human is re-wired to forget as part of its initiation into the shared social, political and economic worlds. But even simple things, like the experience of the beauty of a sunset, reminds us of this loss. And it haunts us, everywhere we go and through everything we do. It even appears in our entertainment.

John But how is any of this possible? You say I emerge out of this metaphysical river yet I can become oblivious to it. It pours into me and yet I misread its messages and signs. That doesn't make sense.

George That's one of the paradoxes of our life. We can cut ourselves off from the source of our life. How else was the barbarity of the Nazi Holocaust possible? How else were millions spellbound by Stalin or are by some terrorist mastermind? For wasn't the monotheist Satan, an angel whose primal act was one of self-severance?

John Why should we be so destructive?

George According to Westhampton University if our social, political and economic forms are premised in such a way that the one demand they make of you is an act of self-severance – the psychoanalytical act of symbolic castration – that is all that is required to wound ourselves and sever our experiences from the fabric of life.

John But how?

George It's complicated. Without a doubt Wittgenstein and William James were right when they said our inner preoccupations are wired into the social, political and economic realities we inhabit. We are mired in the endless imaginary that floats around these corrupted social, political and economic forms. Our nature is distorted, this flow within us is badly warped and distorted. This is in the education at Westhampton. It has to be. These are profound questions about our inner spiritual nature and the social structures we inhabit.

John Are you saying, through the power of negation, avoidance, rejection, or severing things and people of meaning, we have the power to fracture our own souls, the form which organises the flow from the root of the cosmos into our body and mind?

George Yes, and that is why I think we create the conditions which allow totalitarianism, violence and cruelty to grow. That is why I think we create the world in which the human is subsumed under its systems and becomes a variable in a complex algorithm or calculating machine. And those are the conditions which crush education and the imagination, making it almost impossible to believe that there is an alternative to capitalism.

George stood.

John Enough? We have more work to do but that's enough for a start.

George Let's stop. Perhaps we can come back to this in the summer? I have things I must get on with.

John nodded. Everyone closed notebooks, folders and quietly departed. I remained seated for a short time. Two students passed by.

There was a strange atmosphere in the group. So much had been discussed. It was clear there was more to discuss and more to work out, that George had barely scratched the surface of an alternative education. But it was a start.

Contemporary culture has eliminated both the concept of the public and the figure of the intellectual. Former public spaces – both physical and cultural – are now either derelict or colonized by advertising. A cretinous anti-intellectualism presides, cheerled by expensively educated hacks in the pay of multinational corporations who reassure their bored readers that there is no need to rouse themselves from their interpassive stupor. The informal censorship internalized and propagated by the cultural workers of late capitalism generates a banal conformity that the propaganda chiefs of Stalinism could only ever have dreamt of imposing. Zer0 Books knows that another kind of discourse – intellectual without being academic, popular without being populist – is not only possible: it is already flourishing, in the regions beyond the striplit malls of so-called mass media and the neurotically bureaucratic halls of the academy. Zer0 is committed to the idea of publishing as a making public of the intellectual. It is convinced that in the unthinking, blandly consensual culture in which we live, critical and engaged theoretical reflection is more important than ever before.

ZERO BOOKS

If this book has helped you to clarify an idea, solve a problem or extend your knowledge, you may like to read more titles from Zero Books. Recent bestsellers are:

Capitalist Realism Is there no alternative?
Mark Fisher
An analysis of the ways in which capitalism has presented itself as the only realistic political-economic system.
Paperback: November 27, 2009 978-1-84694-317-1 $14.95 £7.99.
eBook: July 1, 2012 978-1-78099-734-6 $9.99 £6.99.

The Wandering Who? A study of Jewish identity politics
Gilad Atzmon
An explosive unique crucial book tackling the issues of Jewish Identity Politics and ideology and their global influence.
Paperback: September 30, 2011 978-1-84694-875-6 $14.95 £8.99.
eBook: September 30, 2011 978-1-84694-876-3 $9.99 £6.99.

Clampdown Pop-cultural wars on class and gender
Rhian E. Jones
Class and gender in Britpop and after, and why 'chav' is a feminist issue.
Paperback: March 29, 2013 978-1-78099-708-7 $14.95 £9.99.
eBook: March 29, 2013 978-1-78099-707-0 $7.99 £4.99.

The Quadruple Object
Graham Harman
Uses a pack of playing cards to present Harman's metaphysical system of fourfold objects, including human access, Heidegger's indirect causation, panpsychism and ontography.
Paperback: July 29, 2011 978-1-84694-700-1 $16.95 £9.99.

Weird Realism Lovecraft and Philosophy
Graham Harman
As Hölderlin was to Martin Heidegger and Mallarmé to Jacques
Derrida, so is H.P. Lovecraft to the Speculative Realist philoso-
phers.
Paperback: September 28, 2012 978-1-78099-252-5 $24.95 £14.99.
eBook: September 28, 2012 978-1-78099-907-4 $9.99 £6.99.

Sweetening the Pill or How We Got Hooked on Hormonal Birth
Control
Holly Grigg-Spall
Is it really true? Has contraception liberated or oppressed
women?
Paperback: September 27, 2013 978-1-78099-607-3 $22.95 £12.99.
eBook: September 27, 2013 978-1-78099-608-0 $9.99 £6.99.

Why Are We The Good Guys? Reclaiming Your Mind From The
Delusions Of Propaganda
David Cromwell
A provocative challenge to the standard ideology that Western
power is a benevolent force in the world.
Paperback: September 28, 2012 978-1-78099-365-2 $26.95 £15.99.
eBook: September 28, 2012 978-1-78099-366-9 $9.99 £6.99.

The Truth about Art Reclaiming quality
Patrick Doorly
The book traces the multiple meanings of art to their various
sources, and equips the reader to choose between them.
Paperback: August 30, 2013 978-1-78099-841-1 $32.95 £19.99.

Bells and Whistles More Speculative Realism
Graham Harman
In this diverse collection of sixteen essays, lectures, and inter-
views Graham Harman lucidly explains the principles of

Speculative Realism, including his own object-oriented philosophy.
Paperback: November 29, 2013 978-1-78279-038-9 $26.95 £15.99.
eBook: November 29, 2013 978-1-78279-037-2 $9.99 £6.99.

Towards Speculative Realism: Essays and Lectures Essays and Lectures
Graham Harman
These writings chart Harman's rise from Chicago sportswriter to co founder of one of Europe's most promising philosophical movements: Speculative Realism.
Paperback: November 26, 2010 978-1-84694-394-2 $16.95 £9.99.
eBook: January 1, 1970 978-1-84694-603-5 $9.99 £6.99.

Meat Market Female flesh under capitalism
Laurie Penny
A feminist dissection of women's bodies as the fleshy fulcrum of capitalist cannibalism, whereby women are both consumers and consumed.
Paperback: April 29, 2011 978-1-84694-521-2 $12.95 £6.99.
eBook: May 21, 2012 978-1-84694-782-7 $9.99 £6.99.

Translating Anarchy The Anarchism of Occupy Wall Street
Mark Bray
An insider's account of the anarchists who ignited Occupy Wall Street.
Paperback: September 27, 2013 978-1-78279-126-3 $26.95 £15.99.
eBook: September 27, 2013 978-1-78279-125-6 $6.99 £4.99.

One Dimensional Woman
Nina Power
Exposes the dark heart of contemporary cultural life by examining pornography, consumer capitalism and the ideology of women's work.

Paperback: November 27, 2009 978-1-84694-241-9 $14.95 £7.99.
eBook: July 1, 2012 978-1-78099-737-7 $9.99 £6.99.

Dead Man Working

Carl Cederstrom, Peter Fleming

An analysis of the dead man working and the way in which capital is now colonizing life itself.

Paperback: May 25, 2012 978-1-78099-156-6 $14.95 £9.99.
eBook: June 27, 2012 978-1-78099-157-3 $9.99 £6.99.

Unpatriotic History of the Second World War

James Heartfield

The Second World War was not the Good War of legend. James Heartfield explains that both Allies and Axis powers fought for the same goals - territory, markets and natural resources.

Paperback: September 28, 2012 978-1-78099-378-2 $42.95 £23.99.
eBook: September 28, 2012 978-1-78099-379-9 $9.99 £6.99.

Find more titles at www.zero-books.net